G000254579

PEERLESS PUNCHESTOWN

150 Years *of* Glorious Tradition

ACKNOWLEDGMENTS

Regrettably, Raymond Smith died in early April 2000 as this publication was being concluded. It would not have been possible but for the tremendous co-operation and assistance which he received from so many people, notably those who supplied photographs and historic material - including the Leinster Leader Punchestown supplements - those whom he interviewed and those who assisted him in any way.

He appreciated the professionalism of Eamon Sinnott & Partners, Graphic Design Studio, Naas and John Hick of the Brookfield Printing Company, Dublin. Most of all we would like to thank Charles Murless, Chief Executive Punchestown Racecourse and James Osborne, Chairman.

Thanks to the following who contributed photographs or other assistance in the compilation of this book. Baroness de Robeck, Major John de Burgh, Mr. Shane Lawlor, Mr. Tom MacGinnty, Ms. Anne Maria Heskin, Mr. Ned Byrne, Mr. Jimmy Grainger, Mr. Patrick Guinness, Mrs. Avril Whitehead, Ms. Anne Fitzsimons, Mr. Stan Hickey, Ms. Karl Kiely, Ms. Colette O'Daly, National Library, Mr. Michael Kavanagh, The Leinster Leader Ltd., Kildare County Council and the Manager, The Shelbourne Hotel, Dublin.

Punchestown Conyngham Cup 1872
The Stone Wall - Opposite Title Page
The Double Bank - Opposite Page 214
Printed by J. Sturgess
Engraved by E. G. Hester

PEERLESS PUNCHESTOWN

150 Years *of* Glorious Tradition

RAYMOND SMITH AND CON COSTELLO

Published on behalf of Punchestown Racecourse

by Sporting Books Publishers, Dublin

Sponsored by Heineken Ireland Ltd.

First Published April, 2000

Copyright © Raymond Smith, 2000

Copyright © Con Costello, 2000

ISBN: 0-9526674-5-2

Other books by Raymond Smith:

Vincent O'Brien: The Master of Ballydoyle (1991)
The High Rollers of the Turf (1992)
Tigers of the Turf (1994)
Vincent O'Brien: The Man and the Legend (1997)
The High Rollers of the Turf: Millennium Edition (1999)
Urbi et Orbi and all that (1995)

Published on behalf of Punchestown Racecourse

by Sporting Books Publishers, Dublin

Printed by Brookfield Press, Dublin

Designed by Eamon Sinnott & Partners, Naas

CONTENTS

FOREWORD BY THE MINISTER FOR FINANCE, MR. CHARLIE MCCREEVY T.D.

I am happy to have the honour of writing the Foreword to the history of Punchestown by Raymond Smith and Con Costello, appropriately titled *Peerless Punchestown: 150 Years of Glorious Tradition.*

It is fitting that it should be launched to coincide with the 150th birthday of the course at its present location and that, now at last, there will be a permanent record of the development from small beginnings of the Spring meeting into the great national and international four-day Festival it is today.

In 1998 I was privileged to open officially the new £8.75 million complex that meant in effect a 'new Punchestown'. That I performed that ceremony on 'Walking Sunday' had a depth of significance for me, almost impossible to put into words. For the racing fraternity, the Spring Punchestown Festival is important and unique. But for native Kildare folk it means an awful lot more. It is not just a race meeting; tradition is part and parcel of Punchestown, and 'Walking Sunday' is an integral part of that tradition.

Then the races themselves, two days until 1963 when it developed into a three-day meeting, and eventually became a four-day Festival in 1999 with pronounced success. The 'outside', as the popular free area was known, was my world and that of my pals in childhood and youthful days. So much to remember that can never fade from the mind.

Now Punchestown has advanced to a new stage of development, with even more ambitious plans for further development in the years ahead. I offer them my personal congratulations for all that has been achieved in a comparitvely short time, and congratulations also to Raymond Smith and Con Costello for giving us such a fine and timely record of the history of the course.

Charlie McCreevy Minister for Finance

Message from the Chairman

Racing began at Punchestown in 1850 and thus we are celebrating our 150th Festival Meeting. Throughout those years of not inconsiderable change to both society and the environment, Punchestown has managed, due to the endeavours of many, to improve and prosper whilst still retaining its unique location and character. Indeed I believe its future has never looked better.

The Directors of Punchestown were anxious that the occasion should not pass without recognition and we are extremely grateful to Raymond Smith and Con Costello for writing the official history and to Heineken and the other sponsors who have made this book possible.

It is fitting that the book should be published in the year 2000 when the course celebrates its 150th anniversary, and fitting also that it should be available for sale during the Festival.

James Osborne
Chairman

EDITORS NOTE

Ever since I first started attending the Punchestown Festival meeting I have been fascinated by the history and traditions of the course.

So I was honoured when James Osborne (Chairman) and Charles Murless (Chief Executive) asked me to combine with Con Costello, well-known Kildare historian, in the writing of the history, the idea being that it would be ready for Punchestown 2000.

This does not profess to be an exhaustive, detailed history, rather it is a celebration of horse and man, a celebration too of epoch-making moments and legends that have lived down the decades and will always be discussed whenever Punchestown itself comes up in conversation.

The old historic prints add immensely, to the lasting value of the book, which will, we trust, be on the bookshelf of everyone who values Punchestown's unique traditions, and that the book will bring back many happy memories to the people of County Kildare and its environs who have enjoyed 'Walking Sunday', and all the fun of the fair, as kids, on the outside or popular area of the course.

Raymond Smith

The Directors and staff of Punchestown greatly regret that Raymond Smith died during the final stages of the production of *Peerless Punchestown - 150 Years of Glorious Tradition*. His enthusiasm, professionalism and thorough understanding of National Hunt racing, its origins and its history are unmistakably apparent in the quality of the finished book. His dedication to the completion of this unique and historic project is very much appreciated by everyone who had been involved with this project.

Charles Murless Chief Executive

MESSAGE FROM THE MANAGING DIRECTOR OF MURPHY BREWERY IRELAND

Heineken is delighted to sponsor the history of what has become a great racing tradition, the Punchestown National Hunt Festival.

Over the last 150 years, the Punchestown National Hunt Festival has successfully grown to become a firm favourite on the sporting and social calendar for racing enthusiasts and supporters, as well as members of the general public who simply want to enjoy the fantastic atmosphere which surrounds the week-long Festival. Indeed it is often referred to as 'Ireland's Cheltenham'.

Heineken, through its sponsorship of the Punchestown Heineken Gold Cup, has enjoyed a great association with the Punchestown National Hunt Festival. In acknowledging the premium stature of the event, Heineken was delighted to increase its prize fund in the Punchestown Heineken Gold Cup to £120,000 last year; thus making it the richest race of the Festival.

On behalf of my colleagues in Murphy Brewery, I would like to take this opportunity to formally acknowledge and commend our friends at Punchestown on the outstanding development programme which has been implemented and completed to the highest standards. There is no doubt that the investment in Punchestown has made it one of the finest racing tracks in the country, with state of the art spectator and hospitatilty facilities.

Racing and hunting have remained proud traditions for many generations of Irish people. This year's Punchestown National Hunt Festival is particularly significant as it is the first meeting of the new Millennium. I am confident that all associated with Punchestown will remain focussed on keeping the Festival spirit alive and preserve the uniqueness of the Nation's annual National Hunt Festival.

Padraic Liston
Managing Director, Murphy Brewery Ireland

ACCEPT A PEOPLES WELCOME

WHEN A KING WENT RACING AT PUNCHESTOWN...
*The Prince of Wales made his first visit to Punchestown in 1868,
drawing a vast crowd of 150,000. He returned as King Edward VII
in 1904 with the Queen and their daughter, Princess Victoria,
County Kildare gave him a truly Royal welcome as this banner
across the main street in Naas clearly indicates.*

Introduction

PEERLESS PUNCHESTOWN
- A TRADITION FEW OTHER RACECOURSES
CAN MATCH

From the Big Banks and Stone Wall Era to be acclaimed nowadays as the 'Irish Cheltenham'

Raymond Smith

Raymond Smith looks at the depth of tradition behind the Punchestown racecourse, which is unparalleled in many ways, and pinpoints how it developed from the era of the famous Big Double and stone wall obstacles to be acclaimed today as the 'Irish Cheltenham'.

The traditions go deep, deeper than any historian could have imagined as he sets out to decipher what created the uniqueness of Punchestown and how it overcame all vicissitudes to win undisputed recognition as Ireland's National Hunt Festival and, more than that, an ever-increasing influx of lovers of the jumping game from Britain and visitors from the Continent and other parts of the globe as well.

When today you move about the spacious £8.75 million complex, officially opened by Minister for Finance, Charlie McCreevy T.D. in 1998, remember that 150 years ago, spectators had only a limited view of the racing as there was as yet no Stand. Punchestown after all, was being established as a permanent venue in the post-Famine year of 1850, though Co. Kildare was not hit as badly by the Great Hunger as other parts of the country.

A combination of many factors came together to ensure that Punchestown would generate in the Spring an intense attraction that resulted in it becoming a Mecca for the people of Dublin, and at the same time attracting racing enthusiasts from all parts of the country, while it was holiday time in no uncertain fashion for the families of Kildare and other surrounding counties.

THE BIG DOUBLE...
The size and scale and challenge presented by the Big Double in the old days is graphically captured in this print. The number of horses that could 'fly' it could be counted on the fingers of two hands

But overshadowing all else, I feel, was the fact that it was a 'people's Festival' from the outset. The famous pictures of the 'outside' as the popular free area was known, prove this beyond any shadow of doubt.

As Charlie McCreevy has so aptly put it... "this was our world in childhood days when I first started attending Punchestown and it was the world of all my school-pals, including Michael Sheerin (now Editor of the *Leinster Leader*). Here we could enjoy all the fun of the fair from the swings to the hurdy-gurdys and the dodgems..."

OVER THEY GO...
Sailing over
the stone wall.

"I recall the Army personnel keeping back the crowds with a rope as there were no railings then. That went on for a long time. And the link with the Kildare Hunt has been kept with the huntsmen leading out the runners for each race".

"I remember when it was normal to have a bet of one shillings, and 2/6 (half-a-crown) on the Tote was a 'fierce' wager. I have seen the changes that have come to Punchestown. I have watched its growth with great interest and with a sense of pride born out of never wanting to miss it from those childhood and youthful times on the 'outside'".

"I associate Punchestown to this day with the smell of chips - chips like you got them nowhere else. It was a time when freedom - the freedom of the open spaces - sang in our hearts and it was a world we would not have exchanged for anything".

"It was then, I suppose, that a love of horses and racing and a flutter on one's fancy was ingrained in me and became an integral part of my life. We would watch the field swing past the Stand coming towards the up-bank fence and I have a memory of horses being killed there, their backs or legs broken when they could not negotiate it safely".

The rejection of exclusivity - the exclusivity of the Royal Enclosure at Ascot's June meeting, for example - has always been one of the strengths of Punchestown. People from all walks of life rub shoulders together in the enclosures and on the stands, the common bond being a shared love of National Hunt racing. You can walk up to a Cabinet Minister and say: 'Well, what do you fancy in the third?' and he will not be in the least fazed, for as the late Terry Rogers used put it - 'all men are equal over and under the Turf'.

The English can never quite get the hang of this easy informality between high-profile politicians and ordinary every-day folk when it comes to an Irish race-meeting. They create for themselves certain barriers that never come down. And in a way they envy us for a singular ethos that is as racy as the very soil itself. Long may it be thus.

In the days before Ireland attained its freedom, very close links were established between the military and Punchestown. It was the era when famous regiments like the Royal Horse Artillery, the Dragoon Guards and the Royal Irish Lancers were stationed at the Curragh and other centres. The military races attracted officers not alone from within the county but from garrisons everywhere, providing rare spectacles.

During the Boer War and the First World War the military races were suspended for a time because officers and men based in Kildare were away fighting at the front.

Amazingly, the meeting went ahead in 1916, and what was most noticeable of all that year was the number of officers home on leave from the trenches who really entered into the spirit of things because deep down they knew that once they went back to the killing fields of Flanders and the Somme, they might not return. Some rode in the races - attacking the stone wall and banks as fearlessly as they would the enemy trenches.

RETURNING FROM PUNCHESTOWN IN 1868... and what was then for many a mandatory stop at the Blackchurch Inn for 'refreshments'.

Punchestown and the Military

The military certainly brought great colour, atmosphere and gaiety to the meeting. Regiments made it a point of vying with each other in dispensing free hospitality in specially erected marquees. The British Forces departed with the establishment of the Free State. However, the tradition of dispensing hospitality in keeping with the old days was maintained by the Irish Army. Indeed, the close association between the Irish Army and Punchestown continued very strongly and would be welded with the passing years.

The mid-19th century, when Punchestown was establishing itself as the premier jumping meeting in the country, coincided with the era when racing horses was for the sporting aristocracy - the 'gentry' - and yet even then the populace loved the chases.

It coincided too with the era when Punchestown became associated with lavish parties that were given plenty of column inches in the newspapers of the time and, of course, a special spotlight was turned on the Hunt Ball - held in Naas - that was a really grandiose affair.

A Great Social Occasion

But overshadowing all else was the manner in which Punchestown became a magnet for two days in the Spring. To miss it was as unthinkable for thousands just as it would seem unthinkable for those lovers of the Cheltenham Festival scene to fail to make the great March meeting nowadays.

The arrival of the motor car was as yet quite a distance over the horizon. Horse-drawn vehicles were the norm and can you imagine it - those domiciled in Dublin in a position to do so would send relief horses down to centres like Rathcoole where they were stabled overnight. The train from Dublin to Sallins brought those who could not afford a cab or other means of road transport. People didn't seem to mind being inconvenienced once they got there eventually. They even went by train from Dublin with intermediate stops along the way to the Hunt Ball in Naas and returned at 3.30. a.m., quite a few missing the train as it seemed too early to allow the fun to end!

Baroness de Robeck of Gowran Grange, close to Punchestown recalls a field below the house which would have been chock-full with horse-drawn cabs and wagonettes of every conceivable kind. She even remembers being told of a hearse with plumed horses that had been pressed into service to meet the demands of Punchestown.

THE IRISH LIFE
*Pictures from the 'Course at Punchestown'
as featured in Irish Life, 1st May 1912.*

Could there be any greater indication of its importance in the racing social calendar? Baroness de Robeck recalled for me the days when the house teemed with guests for the duration of the two-day meeting. 200 to 300 people would be invited to afternoon tea after the races. Many of these would then proceed to different house parties or out to dinner with friends.

Still retained to this day in Gowran Grange are the name pennants that adorned the sandwiches - anchovy sandwiches being a speciality!

A Great Tidal Wave

Business concerns closed down throughout Kildare to facilitate their employees. Nothing was more important than the races. In the early days of the century it was the custom for the majority of the big business houses in Dublin to close for the second day of the meeting. Even public Boards in the metropolis were adjourned for the day and the flow of people heading from Dublin towards Punchestown became like a great tidal wave.

When the weather was particularly dry, blinding dust clouds rose from the roads causing the ladies to think only of protecting their new outfits and the men to stop along the way to quench their thirst ('two large ones quick and two sherries for the ladies!'). When they arrived at the course, men and women looked like veritable phantoms, with dust covering their clothes, hats and faces.

The bicycle was still a key means of conveyance. Naas was thronged the night before the Festival meeting as it was thronged right through the meeting. About 100 men of the old R.I.C. were on duty. One heard voices from every corner of Ireland.

Famous Dublin Gap

The Dublin jarveys battled with the outside horse-drawn vehicles to gain entrance to the racecourse and the sole entrance was through the famous Dublin Gap. It created its own scenes of veritable chaos but still they all managed to get into the course - eventually.

Families gravitated towards the free part of the course or 'outside' area because it was there that the kids could have the time of their lives. Again granted the day was fine and the rain held off, they would pick a spot near the famous *Big Double Bank* complete

ES SNACKS

ALL THE FUN OF THE FAIR...
These kids are grown up now but they will
still remember the joy and excitement they experienced
on the day this picture was taken in 1983.

King Carnival ruled

Much of the long-standing tradition associated with Punchestown sprang from what was created in the 'outside' as it came simply to be known. King Carnival ruled joyously and completely. Here was captured the old spirit of Irish merry-making. Here too were to be found the strolling musicians, the three-card-trick men, discreetly veiled and tented fortune-tellers, men of the roads, strong men performing prodigious feats of strength and endurance, street singers, dwarfs and a host of others, all combining to create a bedlam which oddly enough went unnoticed by those caught up in the racing itself.

Pulse of Punchestown

It was 'outside' that the pulse of Punchestown beat. You could partake of a 'Punchestown sandwich' (topweight) and a creamy pint (the favourite for money) and one writer of that earlier era concluded that if you hadn't savoured the unique brand of humour and entertainment that permeated these open spaces on the course, then you had missed something that was peculiarly Irish, as no-one knows better than the Irish how to create the *craic* and keep it going.

with the picnic basket where after he had partaken of his repast, Dad could slip away to exchange tit-bits of information with companions before having a wager.

The simplicity of life was in the shared joy of what Punchestown could offer on so many different planes. The Celtic Tiger and the constant ringing of mobile phones would have represented another world to these families should they be transported through the time barrier to see how the whiz-kids especially those in the financial services sector live their pressure-cooker lives to-day.

"Celebration of the Horse"

It was truly a 'celebration of the horse' in the National Hunt sphere and it was from the outset a people's Festival in the sense that there were no barriers to the mingling of city dwellers with their country cousins.

So, as one can see, the bedrock of Punchestown's glorious traditions stemmed from this annual occasion offering something special to all men from all walks of life. I find when I go there each year what was created down the decades from as far back as 1850 seems in a strange way to permeate the very atmosphere to this day. It adds an uniqueness to the meeting similar for me, to the uniqueness offered at Cheltenham.

Such has been the success story surrounding Punchestown from its growth beyond the big banks and stone-wall era to add bush fences and hurdles and eventually Flat racing that it was inevitable that it would have to expand its facilities to meet the demands imposed by ever-growing attendances.

Thus Punchestown went forward into the new Millennium with an imposing new stand complex and other amenities costing a total of £8.75 million. Charles Murless, Chief Executive of Punchestown, was at pains to emphasise to me that the preservation of the atmosphere that has made it so appealing to racegoers was uppermost in the minds of the directors as they made their development plans.

CHANGING TIMES...
The paddock and parade ring in 1938 (left) and (above right) how it has all changed with the advent of the new £8.75m complex in 1998.

Epoch-Making Meeting

The new stand, like other new stands in sporting arenas today, has its private suites and these are essential in ensuring that a complex does not mean a crippling burden of debt. But again the Punchestown management does not see this as in anyway affecting the overall atmosphere engendered by its Festival meeting.

The Spring Festival meeting in the year 2000 became an epoch-making one in its own right as it marked the 150th. anniversary of the historic moment when the Kildare Hunt Club chose Punchestown as the permanent venue for their annual meeting. Yes, 1850 was the year when all really began. And then in 1854 another

barrier was broken when the first two-day meeting was held at the new permanent venue that Punchestown had now become.

By 1861 the steeplechasing programme comprised seven races including the National Hunt Steeplechase over three and a half miles for what was then the biggest prize put up for a race in Ireland - £300 added to a £5 sweepstake.

The Kildare Hunt Club had always been planning for the day when it would find a permanent home. Initially races were held wherever a suitable course seemed to present itself. Thus there are records of races at Rathgorrah, excellent racing country just south of Kill Hill, and every yard and every fence could be seen from the hill.

Many Sportsmen's or Red Coat Races, as well as Regimental Races, were staged over this same course. Other meetings were held at Kilcock, at Corbally Harbour, at Burnt Furze (under Furness Wood), at Rathcoole and at Naas (which, however, only consisted of Flat racing.)

The First Meeting

The first meeting, of which a definite record was kept, was held in 1824 over two days. The next seems to have been in 1827 which went on for no less than four days. In 1828 they managed to make up a programme for five days. There is a mention of as many as five races for a one-day meeting in 1830.

Significantly, it was at such local meetings that steeplechasing in Ireland took its origins and had its roots established. In 1837 there was a major break-through with the presentation of a Cup by the Kildare Hunt to be run for annually. It was the era when such races were run in heats over natural country, and spectators followed the race on foot or on horseback. The first official record of the Kildare Hunt Cup reads: 'The Kildare Hunt Steeplechase: Two miles over a sporting country'. It was won by Zephyr, owned by Mr. Lynch.

Broke New Ground

The Kildare Hunt broke new ground in 1842 by running its steeplechase without heats, according to Brian Smith in his beautifully produced book, *The Horse in Ireland*.

In 1845 Mr. Alexander R. Kirkpatrick of Donacomper, Celbridge won the Kildare Hunt Cup on Pilgrim, a horse blind in one eye, in a field of three, Mr. de Burgh's Grosette being second and his Swindler third.

An amazing feature of that time was the fact that the 1840's saw steeplechasing flourish in Ireland despite the Great Hunger - the terrible famine years, which saw an estimated million people die from starvation and fever. The population dropped from eight million in 1841 to six-and-a-half million ten years later. They left in their thousands in the 'coffin ships' for the States, hoping to find happiness and prosperity in a brave New World.

After the departure of the British Army and the establishment of the Irish Free State, the Irish Army maintained the long traditional links with the Punchestown Festival meeting. Army horses shown here on parade in front of the stand in 1999.

Populace Loved the Chase

Horse-racing, as we have seen, was for the sporting aristocracy. Yet, the populace too, loved the excitement of the chase. Lord Clonmell, who became Master of the Kildares in 1852, may not have been a noted rider but he created his own niche in Punchestown history. Mounted on his favourite white horse and resplendent in the scarlet uniform of the Kildare Hunt Club, he would canter up and down the rails carrying a thong whip in his right hand and, as one observer of the time described it, 'cheerily berating the rustics with whom, as with those of his own rank, he is an equal favourite.'

It was in 1850 that the advantage of the course at Punchestown attracted the attention of the Kildare Hunt members, who from that year onwards adopted this incomparable terrain as the permanent place for their annual meeting.

It is generally agreed that the Punchestown meeting owed much of its success in the early years to the Corinthian Cup, first competed for on March 28 1853. The Cup was put up by Captain, the Honourable William Hely-Hutchinson, who was a son of Lord Donoughmore.

The initial winner was a horse called The Squire, ridden to victory by his owner Mr. Peter Wilkins, veterinary surgeon with the 11th. Hussars.

In a field of seventeen he came home ahead of Lord Howth's Poacher, the mount of Mr. Trench Nugent, while in third place was Mr. C. Lyons's, Don Juan, ridden by Mr. Billy Hutchinson. Only a neck separated first and second and a half-a-length the second and third.

William Hely-Hutchinson, known affectionately as 'Billy' by his friends was a noted character in his own right. He was 'Keeper' of the staghounds of the 11th Hussars and was the right-hand man of the immortal Sam Reynell's in 'the making of the Meath country'.

The personalities who rode in the Corinthian Cup race were sportsmen to their finger-tips and courageous to a fault. They gloried in the challenge of the chase and in the individual cross-country matches that were a precursor of all that was to follow in the jumping sphere. In some instances if a man managed to survive a killer fall in a chase, he died in battle in wars in which life represented cheap fodder for the guns.

Many of the leading figures in the Irish steeplechasing world feature in the famous picture by Michael Angelo Hayes RHA of the participants in the Corinthian Cup at Punchestown in 1854.

Captain Hely-Hutchinson, who won the race on Torrent, would die subsequently of 'camp fever' in the Crimean War; Captain Wombwell A.D.C. who had two horses killed under him in the Charge of the Light Brigade, fell into Russian hands and then, amazingly, managed to vault on to a loose horse and regained his own lines.

In the picture also were officers from the 16th Lancers, the 2nd and 7th Dragoon Guards and the 11th Hussars. Depicted too was the Marquis of Waterford who had the distinction twelve years earlier of staging a great steeplechase - the New Melton Stakes - in the area around the village of New Inn between Cahir and Cashel in County Tipperary. He laid out the course over his own lands and the evening before the race he gave a dinner party for 120 guests.

Michael Angelo Hayes's renowned study of the Corinthian Cup at Punchestown 1854 depicts sixth from left the Marquis of Drogheda 'Mr Punchestown'; eight from left in foreground, horse's head lowered, Capt J. W. Billy Hely Hutchinson, who rode Torrent to Victory that day, but died later of 'camp fever' in the Crimean War, eleventh from left the Marquis of Waterford, beside J. G. Price of the Second Dragoons on his distinctive grey, and twenty-third from left in background right, on a grey horse Capt. Wombwell who survived the Charge of The Light Brigade in the most amazingly courageous fashion.

Ideal Testing Ground

For trainers and owners, Punchestown was viewed well over a century-and-a-half ago as the ideal testing ground for potential Grand National contenders. The banks and ditches demanded natural jumping ability and courage, and it was reckoned that the horse that could triumph here could conquer the Aintree fences.

Irish-bred Ambush 11, carrying the colours of the Prince of Wales, took the Maiden Plate at Punchestown in 1898 and two years later won the Aintree Grand National. Other notable National winners who cut their teeth, so to speak, by winning at Punchestown were Workman (1939) and Lovely Cottage(1946). It was to the latter that the immortal Prince Regent failed to give the weight in the 1946 National after winning the Gold Cup that same year.

In the era when it was seen as a great annual point-to-point meeting, Punchestown became the battle-ground where potential stars from various Hunts pitted their talents against each other over the famous banks. Pictures extant from that era of action in the Conyngham Cup and Prince of Wales Plate bear witness to the wealth of tradition and the mystique surrounding the Festival itself.

The First Stand

Punchestown was conscious of the need to cater for spectators long before many other courses in Ireland had awakened to the fact.

Back in the 1860's permanent stands were erected and enclosures laid out. In this, Punchestown was giving the lead in the National Hunt arena. Up to then, chasing was viewed as a sport in which gentlemen could indulge and which they could organise for themselves. The needs of the ordinary spectators did not command urgent attention and certainly not the expenditure of money.

But Ireland could not but be influenced by events in Britain. As racing there entered the commercial era with the advent of enclosed park courses leading in turn to greatly-improved facilities and to increased betting activity, the knock-on effect was evident on the other side of the Irish Sea. New courses in Galway (1869) and Leopardstown (1888) would revolutionise the scene and, in the case of Leopardstown, the erection of artificial fences allied to shorter races indicated clearly that the era of the old cross-country matches was finally buried.

Into the Modern Era

In time too, the big banks and stone wall at Punchestown were modified, and park-course National Hunt racing and Flat racing would bring the course into the modern era. Later still, generous sponsorship would mean races that attracted more English raiders, who added to the intensity of the rivalry for these prestigious prizes.

But Punchestown would never break entirely with its sacrosanct tradition. It would retain races that in their very names were indicative of its glorious past and the immortal personalities who graced the scene down the decades.

Glance down the programme and you will still see holding a place of pride, The La Touche Cup over 4m. 1f. and 33 fences in all. And there's still the Hunters Chase for the Ladies Perpetual Cup over 3m. and 21 fences for four-year-olds and upwards and the Champion Certified Hunters Chase for five-year-olds and upwards.

The programme then has an overall balance to satisfy all tastes and in that balance is preserved the core facets of the Punchestown of close on 150 years ago.

In 1999 - the last year of the 20th century - Punchestown broke new ground again by staging its first four-day meeting.

First Four-Day Meeting

Charles Murless and the members of the Committee had the wisdom and the vision to ensure that the fourth day provided racing of the highest quality in the showpiece events like the Shell Champion Hurdle and the David Austin Memorial Chase. The inaugural running of the Shell Champion Hurdle was graced by reigning Smurfit Champion hurdler Istabraq and, naturally, many who had not managed to get to Cheltenham to see him winning his second successive crown were now afforded the opportunity of acclaiming J.P. McManus's champion supreme.

And how the crowd loved it. They were twelve deep round the parade ring and the cheers rang out after Istabraq returned to the No. 1. spot, where Charlie Swan entered into the spirit of the occasion by throwing his whip into the air.

'The best ever' was how James Osborne, Chairman of the Punchestown Development Company Limited summed up the success of Punchestown '99. A majority of the 87,000 racegoers who enjoyed the sun-drenched Festival meeting over the four days heartily echoed those sentiments. The fact that there were eight English-trained winners provided ample proof of what an established favourite the meeting has become with British trainers and with the thousands who had crossed the Irish Sea to attend.

*A crowded stand and the latest fashion
of the day as Punchestown maintains
its singular popularity in 1896.*

1

PUNCHESTOWN
A SPECIAL PLACE IN THE ANNUAL
SOCIAL CALENDAR

Con Costello

Evenings of lavish house parties...the Hunt Ball graced by Royalty... and the races themselves synonymous with the era of the big banks and stone wall fences that presented a special challenge to horse and rider.

In the following chapters the establishment in 1850 of Punchestown at its current venue from inauspicious beginnings to grow into the great Spring National Hunt Festival meeting it has become today is told. It shows how it overcame the agrarian protests of the Land War, the indirect effects of the Boer War and First World War, also the War for Independence and the Civil War to maintain its unique position as a racing Festival that attracted people from all parts of Ireland, holding a special place always in the lives of the people of County Kildare and surrounding counties.

On the Outside in 1868.

The spotlight is put in vivid fashion on the status of the Punchestown meeting in the annual social calendar... on the great house parties that were reported in detail in the newspapers of the day... and nothing, of course, matched the impact of the annual Kildare Hunt Ball that was held for the first time in Naas Town Hall in 1860.

Indeed, so important did Punchestown become with the evolving decades that a bard was inspired to write a 55-verse epic about it.

It inspired also some magnificent paintings, including Michael Angelo Hayes's 1854 water-colour The Corinthian Cup and Charles Hunt's splendid engravings (1856) which show the horses *Charging the Stone Wall* and *Leaping the Rail Bank*. And most famous of all the graphic engravings of the visit of the Prince of Wales in 1868, depicting not alone the Prince mounted on a white steed surrounded by 46 military gentlemen but catching all the atmosphere of the 'outside' or free area of the course, down to the pipe-smoking woman selling oranges and bread and the fiddler and his dog and tambourine-playing daughter.

Some of the epoch-making moments in the history of Punchestown are more fully developed in later chapters, like the mammoth crowd of 150,000 attracted on the day the Prince of Wales went racing, the loss of the first day through snow in 1950 that saw the celebration of the Centenary of Punchestown and the advance into the modern era with the introduction of the bush course in 1960, followed later by the staging of hurdle races on the hallowed turf, then bumpers and ultimately came Flat racing.

A helping hand over a stone wall for a lady in the fashions of the day.

It all Began in 1850

County Kildare has been celebrated as a venue for horse racing since heroic times when the mythological Fionn MacCumhaill and the Fianna raced their horses on the Curragh of Kildare.

In the 17th century the Curragh was described as the Newmarket of Ireland, and in 1790 the Turf Club was established there. Earlier in the 18th century the establishment of the Kildare Hunt Club had confirmed the county as the premier centre in the country for equine sports. The Hunt Club held races in different locations in the county, but the first official record of a Kildare Hunt Steeplechase is from 1837. In the early 1840s races were sometimes held at Punchestown, but the meeting which established it as the regular venue was in the post-Famine year of 1850. It was an ominous start to the holding of the races, which closed the hunting season.

The morning of Monday, 1st April, 1850, according to a report in the *Leinster Express*, "broke hazy and threatening and caused an exceedingly thin attendance from Dublin, the assemblage at Punchestown being chiefly composed of persons from the surrounding neighbourhood". The journalist was not impressed by the arrangements, noting that "they lacked perfection. There was no Stand House, the view of the running was limited, and the course very badly kept. As the day advanced the wind and rain increased in violence, and the sports, which did not commence 'till a quarter past two o'clock, were carried on amid a perfect hurricane. Racing finished at a quarter past five o'clock, the weather continuing boisterous and wet, and the journey back to Dublin being as disagreeable as can well be imagined".

If it was an unpleasant day for the racing correspondent, it was a good day for Thomas de Burgh of Oldtown, Naas, as on Medora he won the Hunt Cup for horses the property of the Kildare Hunt and ridden by same. The continuity and prominence of County Kildare families in the Hunt and steeplechasing was evident in 1948 when Major John de Burgh's Standboy won the Kildare Hunt Plate at Punchestown. He was a great grand-son of the winner of the Hunt Cup in 1850.

Importance of the Military

The importance of the military to the Hunt was confirmed in 1853 when the Corinthian Cup, a Free Handicap of five sovereigns each, with a piece of Plate value £50 added, was instituted. It was for competition between members of the Kildare Hunt, the United Services Club and for horses the property of officers quartered in the Dublin district. Horses were to have been hunted in the season 1852-'53, and ridden by members of one of the above clubs, or by officers on full pay in the army or navy.

The Hon J.W. Hely Hutchinson and Richard Wellesley Bernard, printed in 1854 by Michael Angelo Hayes.

That meeting was described in the *Leinster Express* as "one of the most brilliant affairs we have seen in the vicinity of Dublin for many years, both as regards the quality of the sport and the number and respectability of the visitors. His Excellency the Lord Lieutenant, accompanied by Colonel Pringle A.D.C. to the Queen; Major Bagot, Comptroller; Major Ponsonby and Captain Harvey, arrived from Dublin in an open barouche shortly before the start of the races and proceeded to the Stand House, a portion of which was railed off for the accommodation of His Excellency and suite. His Excellency remained until the races were over, and seemed to take much interest in each race as it was run off".

Initial two-day Fixture

The first two-day meeting at Punchestown in 1854 was immortalised in Michael Angelo Hayes's water-colour The Corinthian Cup. It includes such county worthies as the Earl of Clonmell, Lord Cloncurry, the Marquis of Drogheda, William Kennedy, who was Master of the Kildare Hunt, and Capt. The Hon. J.W. Hely Hutchinson on Torrent, the winner of the Cup. The latter rider, with his cousin Richard Wellesley Bernard on Beware, were also the subject of another painting of that occasion by Hayes. The popularity of Punchestown prompted the artist Charles Hunt to issue a pair of engravings in 1856 which show the horses *Charging The Stone Wall* and *Leaping the Rail Bank*.

First Hunt Ball

On the night of the second day of the meeting in 1860 the first Kildare Hunt Ball was held in Naas Town hall. It was so successful that the proposal was made that "each succeeding season will be brought to a close with as brilliant a re-union as the one we have just recorded".

Before giving a full list of the nobility and gentry who attended the Ball, the *Leinster Express* described the ballroom: "On entering the porch from the carriage-way the visitors were agreeably surprised with the light and gay appearance of the passage, carpeted and tastefully hung with evergreens, flowering shrubs, etc. On entering the hall the brilliant and sprightly lights, which were supplied by Mr Mooney of Ormond Quay, Dublin, first attracted the attention".

This picture of the Crowded Stand in 1896 shows that the popularity of the Punchestown Spring meeting never waned.

The Priests' Hill

There is a famous engraving of 1892
by J. Sturgess showing a number of small
black figures standing on a hill in the distance,
behind the finish of the Conyngham Cup race.
They were the priests who, though keen
followers of the sport, were forbidden
by a Dublin Diocesan Statute of 1862 from
attending race meetings.

Punchestown is in the Archdiocese
of Dublin and the ground they occupied
was known as "The Priests' Hill". It remained
as the venue until that rule was relaxed
in the 1970s. The hill itself was to disappear
in a quarrying operation.

"Ascending the staircase the visitors
were amazed with the magnificence of the
spacious ballroom, hung in pink and white,
with rich festoons, rosettes etc.; over 400
wax lights, in rich ormolu circles and semi-
circles were suspended and hung around
the room, which was tastefully furnished
with sofas, benches etc, ponceau, damask,
immense sized pier glasses, girandolas, and
a superbly fitted up trophy of the Kildare
Hunt, heads, brushes, spurs, whips etc.
adorned one end of the room".

"The Drawing Rooms were gracefully
fitted up and adorned with large and
brilliant plate mirrors. Every attention was
paid to the comfort of guests".

"Shortly after 12 o'clock the spacious
supper room was thrown open. The
appearance of the supper tables was
magnificent. There was the greatest
profusion of every delicacy, and did the
highest credit to the caterer, Mr Ingram
Murphy of 58, York Street, Dublin.
The wines, which were from the cellar
of Mr V. O'Connor, Beresford Place,
Dublin were of the most recherché quality.
Hanlon's well-known band played with great
spirit throughout the evening and gave
the greatest satisfaction".

"There were upwards of 350 persons
at the ball and dancing was kept up until
an advanced hour of the morning. A special
train brought a large number of visitors

from Dublin and intermediate stations along the line, and returned again at half-past three o'clock with a considerably less number than it brought, as several parties did not seem disposed to leave at so early an hour".

Magnetic Telegraph

The racing correspondent from the *Irish Times* in 1863 was able to report by magnetic telegraph that "a score and a half years have now passed since the members of the Kildare Hunt introduced steeplechasing to the wide and far-famed lands of Punchestown" before he gave the results of the day.

Indeed, the popularity of the venue inspired a bard to compose a 55-verse epic, in the course of which he mentioned such Kildare worthies as Lord Naas, the Baron de Robeck, Tom Conolly MP, Aylmer of Donadea and Edward Mansfield "the Hunt's right-hand, a right good fellow he".

Here is one of the verses from the epic:

A loud hurrah for Ireland, boys,
And louder for Kildare,
And loudest of all for Punchestown,
For I know you all are there.

The Bishopscourt Cup

The Kildare Chilling Hunters Steeplechase for the Bishopscourt Cup - the opening race on the opening day of the Festival meeting - has a tremendous significance and importance to the farming community in County Kildare and it has a tradition berhing it as old as the racecourse itself. It's terms are clear - it is confined to "certified hunters of fours years old and upwards owned by farmers, faring land in the Kildare Hunt District".

Down the years it has been a lifetime's ambition of members of the Kildare Hunt to win this race and while professional gamblers of the modern mould may not see it as a betting medium and as it may not help swell the coffers of the Irish Horseracing Authority, it will retain its appeal for those who see it as THE prize to be won and the following it has throughout Kildare means that it will always be an integral part of the Festival programme.

Mr Thomas Conolly

Memorable 1864 Meeting

The euphoria of the journalist who reported the meeting in 1864 was evident in his report: "Twenty-six horses ran in the National Hunt race, horses in blooming condition, eager to be off... the riders dressed in the gayest colours, and their boots, breeches and tops in apple-pie order, some with a couple of inches of brandy on their stomachs. Those gentlemen look jolly and fit for anything, others looking serious, others as if they wish the affair to be over."

The Military Race was described as "a rare specimen of pluck on the part of those gentlemen holding HM commissions, and if they storm the breach or clear the enemy's trenches in the same fashion...

*Viewing the Racing
from the Grand Stand 1896.*

However the Downshire Cup beat by far anything seen in Ireland in the remembrance of the hoariest old bachelor, perhaps in the world such a display never had been witnessed on a racecourse... Punchestown 1864 passed off as a credit to the county in which it was held, and an honour to Old Ireland."

It was estimated that the Great Southern Railway carried over 5, 000 passengers on the two days of the races "without the least inconvenience" to Sallins.

In the following year (1865) the status of the meeting was reflected in an extraordinary attendance of "upwards of 40, 000", and the presence there of correspondents from the *London Times*, the *Morning Post* and the *Daily Express*. The enhancement of the social aspects of Punchestown was apparent in the house parties arranged by the gentry, and in the culmination of the week, the Hunt Ball, which also marked the end of the hunting season.

As a newspaper man enthused: "Every residence in the neighbourhood, from that of peer down to peasant, bore evidence of the approaching meeting for days previous, and every train had the brougham, family omnibus, or private car, awaiting its arrival with the visitors to partake of Kildare hospitality during the meeting and to judge by the highway one could suppose Dublin to be deserted".

Boar's Head on the Menu

The Hunt Ball was again held in Naas Town Hall, which was decorated with evergreens, flowers, bannerettes and armorial devices. Caterers came from Dublin to provide the supper which, in 1867, "included boar's head, Limerick ham, ox tongues, galantines of veal and turkey, peroford pies, soup, salmon, roast chicken and duckling, lobster salads, jellies, creams etc. Mr Hanlon's String Band repertoire included waltzes, quadrilles and the lancers". The newspapers published a comprehensive list of those who attended, including all of the nobility and gentry, and the military officers from the barracks on the Curragh, at Newbridge and Naas, as well as the principal guests in the local house parties.

A decade later the Hunt Ball was an even grander affair as the Duke of Connaught and his retinue were to attend. The ballroom in the Naas Town Hall was redecorated for the ball, and it was reported as being "not unworthy of the groups of fair women and brave men there congregated, *carpe noctem* their motto, as usual Killashee (home of the Moore family) panelled the *spolia opima* and emblems of the chase in a fine trophy. The wines brought pleasant enjoyment without subsequent remorse to the middle man.

His Royal Highness, who seems to have inherited the almost ubiquitous gifts of his family was no mere spectator of the gay scene, and I have no doubt the several plighted youths and maids found the soft glow of wax tapers and the delicious music as pleasing as April's ivory moonlight beneath the chestnut shade of the poet's conception".

Prince and Princess present

In the following year, 1868, the two-day meeting was to be even more exciting and glamourous than usual as the 27-year-old Prince of Wales, who was familiar with Kildare from his period soldiering on the Curragh some years before, was to be present with his Princess.

SPECTATORS IN 1868...
*one of the earliest photographs
of the meeting.*

Hundreds of police were drafted into Naas, where they were accommodated in the Town Hall, to cope with the enormous crowds who were to come by special trains to Sallins - as did the Royal party - and by road. On the racecourse refreshment rooms and other apartments for the visitors had been built at the rear of the Royal Stand, and as the day was glorious and the racing good it was considered a most successful meeting except, as one journalist reported, "for the dreadful music of a German band".

The Grand Military Chase

A regular feature of the two-day meeting was the Irish Grand Military Steeplechase which attracted soldiers not only from within the county, but from garrisons everywhere. Regiments pitched their own tents for dispensing hospitality, and in 1870 "the 65th Carbiniers had a private Stand, with a saloon where they entertained their friends. The State Fusilier Guards and the 43rd Regiment were also encamped on the tented field in a spirit of free hospitality. The band of the Carbiniers played in front of the the Grand Stand and agreeably relieved the monotonous din of the betting ring".

Lieut. Col Charles â Court Repington, who was stationed at the Curragh, nostalgically remembered "the hunting, the race meetings, especially Punchestown".

But he was not there with his mother's approval. She wrote: "I much regret that the occasion should be the races as it naturally strengthens the belief, already too prevalent, that your chief object is amusement". The Prince was not to be deterred, replying: "Dear Mama, that you should fully understand that I do not go there for my amusement, but as a duty". Lord Mayo, he pleaded, had particularly asked him to come.

The *Irish Times* also disapproved: "(The races) held in a wild and inhospitable district, at some distance from a railway station and with but the small town of Naas to afford the accommodation so urgently required for a gathering of such calibre, it would appear the last place to select for a festival so truly national".

WHY THE INCOMPARABLE LADY GALWAY
WAS TREATED LIKE A QUEEN

Lady Galway was the horse that money couldn't buy and which has to be put on a special pedestal in any discussion of the legendary chasers that left an indelible imprint in the history of the Punchestown course.

Lady Galway was, in fact, the fictionalised name of Confederate, owned by Capt. William Tuthill of Moyglare, Maynooth. The gelding had been purchased for £50 in Galway and he was specially trained - and laid out - for the Kildare Hunt Cup. He first won a race that made him eligible for this event.

Now Captain William Tuthill's groom takes up the story: "The Kildare Hunt Cup was the one race in the world that the Captain cared most about winning. I'll explain, so you will understand how they managed this race. It had to be won three years in succession by the same jockey and the same horse if they were both living. If not, they'd have to go back and start all over again (that is if they wanted to keep the trophy).

"The prize was one hundred pounds and a big Gold Cup. The first year (1875) Lady Galway entered this race she won it, ridden by the Hon. Greville Nugent".

"But when the second year come, 'twas the rule that the winning horse of the first race had to carry more pounds for a handicap. The way they did that was to put weights into bags or pockets at the side of the saddle, but that was no bother to Lady Galway, as she won for the second year running".

"The third year she had to carry more weight than the second. They sought the fastest horse they could to defeat her and, in fact, that year Lady Galway ran against the King's own horse but he wasn't swift enough for the little mare. So she won outright the trophy for the Kildare Cup", (presented by Lord Otho FitzGerald).

"There never was such a time at the race track, for no other horse in County Kildare had ever won this famous race before. I heard of lots of people offer Captain Tuthill all sorts of money for Lady Galway, but he said: No, no one's ever going to put a saddle on that mare again and I'll see that they don't, whether I'm living or dead".

"And you couldn't blame the Captain for the honour the mare brought him. After we got back to Moyglare, the Captain took the four shoes off of Lady Galway and sent them away to be silver-mounted, and when they came back, he put them on a shelf in his front hall right over the table where the Gold Cup was kept. And each time I went into the house, same as everyone else, I was always admiring those silver shoes".

"The Captain was true to his word, for he left the mare in a five-acre lot with a running stream at one end of it and he built her a beautiful stall. Like a queen he treated her... So year in and year out Lady Galway lived in clover. I adored that mare, even if she was getting fat and losing her figure".

Note: The real Confederate, a bay gelding, on whom the story of Lady Galway was based won the Kildare Hunt Cup in the colours of Capt. Tuthill three years running, 1873-'75. He was ridden to victory on each occasion by Mr. St. James.

Source: *And that's no lie*.
Beatrice Bill Talbot, Boston 1946

Lavish House Parties

That the house parties for Punchestown were an established part of the social calendar is apparent from the journal kept by John Henry Fock, 4th Baron de Robeck, between 1859 and 1862. In 1859 the guests for Punchestown arrived at Gowran Grange on Monday 11th April, and they enjoyed "very good racing, Aylmer winning everything, the Hunt Cup on the second day". The house party remained at Gowran Grange until the 14th.

In the following year the party arrived on the 16th, and on the following day the Baron noted: "1st day of races, very fine but cold. Two horses killed". But the following day was fine, with good races. Of the Hunt Ball he wrote: "Nothing could have been better. The Town Hall was well got up, the supper excellent, and plenty of people. We kept at it, 'till day light!".

The next evening, at the same venue, the Baron's guests enjoyed a "concert got up by Burgh for the church. Performers all amateurs, went off well". On the 20th April he recorded that: "All the party leave. Finished the hunting season".

Mark Bence-Jones in his book *Twilight of the Ascendancy* tells of the lavish parties given at Bishopscourt in the 1870s by Lord Clonmell: "The host was inclined to do his guests and also himself rather too well.

LORD CLONMELL....
a legend in his own lifetime.

There are many stories told of his exploits when in his cups, such as when Queen Victoria smiled graciously on him at a garden party and he rushed over to her, shook her warmly by the hand and assured her that he knew her face, but could not for the moment remember her name".

Clonmell and some of the other gentry families also entertained in their own tents at Punchestown.

The First Photographs

The first photographs of the Punchestown meeting were taken in 1868, coinciding with the historic visit of the Prince of Wales.

The occasion also marked the making of a splendid engraving from a painting by Henry Barraud. It shows the Prince, mounted on a white steed, surrounded by the county worthies and some forty-six military gentlemen. The Dublin photographer, John Chancellor took the pictures, which included scenes of the ordinary people on the 'outside' watching the racing.

To exploit the demand for images of the Royal visit, Chancellor had autotypes made from his stereo-photographs which were drawn by Mr J.O'Hea, and printed in permanent colours in Scarborough and dedicated to the Marquis of Drogheda. O'Hea drew his impression of the Royal party, their entourage and the crowds of onlookers on gelatine, which was then transferred to soft metallic plates for printing. This combination of photography and drawing produced a splendid souvenir of the day.

In the autotype the Prince is depicted with large groups of recognisable gentlemen standing in front of the Grand Stand, above which flies the Royal flag. The Princess is sitting with her ladies high up on the Stand, beneath The Prince of Wales' Plume. On the left of the Stand there is a group of officers of the Queen's Hussars, and behind the Stand can be seen a couple of marquees, and two regimental tents.

The atmosphere of 'The Outside' is captured in this autotype made by J. O'Hea from Chancellor's stereophotographs taken on the occasion of the visit of the Prince of Wales in 1868.

But it is in the artistically arranged grouping of the animated crowd on the 'outside' that an unique record of the period was recorded. On the left of the picture a *Punch & Judy Show* is in progress, with the drummer summoning the crowd. Arrayed across the front of the picture are all the traditional side-shows, the thimble man, a bookie, a pipe-smoking woman selling oranges and bread to an n.c.o. of the Royal Horse Artillery, a pick-pocket, a ballad singer, the three-card trick man, with two small boys, one smoking, the other eating a pear, beneath his table.

There is a fiddler and his dog, and with his tambourine-playing daughter soliciting alms from the party picnicking on the side-car. Behind the car is a hurdy-gurdy man, and beside it a child selling matches. On the right, behind the man pouring a glass of wine, the two men setting on a wagon are engrossed in something happening out of picture.

PEACE & PROSPERITY.

AND NOT A CAR TO BE SEEN!.. Naas prepares for the Royal visit to Punchestown Races in 1904.

2

THE FIRST TIME PUNCHESTOWN HAD TO BE CANCELLED - AND A DAY OF PANIC IN THE GRANDSTAND

The first time that Punchestown races had to be cancelled was in 1879. That coincided with the commencement of agrarian protests, remembered as the Land War.

Meets of the Kildare Hunt were disrupted and, of course, in the eyes of those who remained aloof from the protests and of the military who saw attendance at the April meeting as a red-letter occasion in the annual social calendar, the idyllic sporting nature of the county was tarnished.

Col. J. R. Harvey, who was serving with the 5th Royal Irish Lancers in Newbridge, later commented: "The country people, even in Kildare, could hardly have been said by their best friends to have done anything this year to maintain that reputation for love of sport generally attributed to the Irish people, and in consequence it was resolved that there should be no Punchestown, a blow felt very much by the people, more especially about Naas, which it may be safely supposed was not without its good effects, though the present loss was ours of course, no hunting meant fewer horses in the regiment, but the card day was very much strengthened by a sporting match and a couple of runs".

The following year the situation was sufficiently calm to permit the holding of the April meeting. And for the next thirty-five years, despite the Boer War and the First World War, there was no interruption of the races, although the military chases were not run for five years due to the absence of the officers at the front. Normally all military training at the Curragh camp was suspended for the two days of the meeting to enable everyone to attend.

But the carnival atmosphere of the race meeting could also be suddenly dissolved.

Most tragic incident

One of the worst and most tragic incidents in the history of Punchestown occurred in the 1870's when someone shouted that the Grand Stand was falling. The crowd panicked and a good number of people were trampled as they stampeded to get down out of the Stand.

A journalist reporting the incident wrote: "If the fellow who had raised the cry which caused the disaster could have been recognised and captured, I should like to have seen him treated as I once did a welsher in the same enclosure. He was stripped to the skin, flogged unmercifully, daubed over with paint, and then kicked out on the course with nothing whatsoever upon him except one boot and a stocking".

In 1864 there had been a collision between two horses close to the finish and when they became entangled in the ropes and posts, they somersaulted into the crowd, killing one spectator and injuring several others. Both riders were knocked unconscious.

The Guinness House Parties

In 1874 Edward Cecil Guinness purchased Farmleigh in County Dublin. There, according to a family historian, he "established a family tradition for large, jolly house parties when, like the rest of their set, they opened their house for the Punchestown Races, the leading event in the Irish social calendar.

"Guinness house parties, however, tended to be bigger and better than the rest. Brimming over with restless energy, the Master of the house occasionally showed off his own accomplished horsemanship, driving a four-hand with relays of horses all the way to Punchestown from St. Stephen's Green".

OUT IN THE COUNTRY... This photograph captures the field out in the country during one of the Punchestown events. Note the old riding style of the jockeys.

A couple of years later it was estimated that from 10, 000 to 12,000 racegoers were present at Punchestown, despite constant rain. The service of a large number of cavalry and police on duty was not called on.

Another Royal Visit

The April meeting of 1885 was another major and social occasion as the Prince and Princess of Wales and their eldest son, Prince Albert Victor, attended. They arrived at the newly-opened railway station at Naas, while the other racegoers coming from Dublin still alighted at Sallins.

But the afternoon of April 21st was a dismal one. The *Irish Times* reported: "Oh, for those shiny hats glistening like mirrors! Alas! for those beautiful bonnets or hats, by whichever name the female headgear is most appropriately denominated. The gloss of those tiles became a matter for history, and all the finery of the ladies was encompassed in wrappings which, as such impedimenta usually do, produced an effect that was in most cases not beautiful".

The reception party for the visitors included Lord Drogheda, the Earl of Mayo, Mr Percy La Touche and Mr Ambrose More O'Ferrall. The racing was not good. The Hunt Cup was won by Mr de Robeck, despite a fall at the first fence.

Silenced by Loud Cheers

The riders were so covered with mud it was difficult to recognise the colours, and the Prince caught a cold and so did not attend the second day. The rain dampened the day, and the attendance was not as great as it had been a decade before for the Prince's first visit to the course. "A few insignificant hisses were heard in the vicinity of the Royal Enclosure which were promptly rebuked and silenced by loud cheers", wrote one observer while another recalled the incident when one young man was knocked to the ground by another punter who shouted: "would you like to hiss the Prince of Wales again?".

If the Prince was unable to grace the second day of the meeting, his heir, Prince Albert did attend.

Just a decade after the visit of the Royal party, Harry Sargent, in his book, *Thoughts on Sport*, noted that: "For thirty years it has been the custom of every cavalry regiment stationed in Ireland at the time, and many of the infantry regiments, to entertain their friends at luncheon during Punchestown. The space set apart for these entertainments is situated, as most people know, at the back of the stand and, covering nearly an acre, is enclosed with corrugated iron paling ten feet high. Within this space some 20 marquees were usually pitched, and in them nearly everyone who had stand tickets got entertained on both days".

Causes Total Solitude

Maria La Touche, the wife of Percy La Touche, was not keen on horses and associated sports, and she appreciated Punchestown as a quiet time when she could concentrate on her gardening. "All the County is concentrated in one spot, which causes total solitude to reign everywhere else. One may wear one's very worst clothes and have earth all over one's hands and tools sticking out of one's pockets, with a peaceful certainty that no visitors will come".

*HOW THE ILLUSTRATED SPORTING
AND DRAMATIC NEWS...
saw the Punchestown Meeting of 1899.*

KILDARE AND NATIONAL HUNT AT PUNCHESTOWN

"THE greatest steeplechase carnival in the world," we in Ireland are accustomed to designate the big Kildare Hunt Meeting at Punchestown; and now the festival, for such it is, has concluded for 1899. I have read all manner of accounts of it, in our Irish daily journals and other literature also; and, truth to tell, have felt reminded of the old saying about men fancying (if able to come out of their graves) that they had got into wrong resting places, judging by eulogistic epitaphs reared over them! Our scribes certainly have indulged in superlatives, and exhausted strings of adulatory adjectives concerning the meeting: "Brilliant weather! healthy breezes! the few short showers not interfering with the comfort of visitors! biggest concourse on record! gigantic improvements everywhere! no more crushing at the 'gap,' no more single-file travelling on roadways too narrow for more extended journeying! gorgeous toilettes, beauty and comfort everywhere!"—and so on, *ad infinitum*.

Good gracious me! rose-coloured spectacles are great institutions for making folks happy and contented, and for ensuring glittering reports of everything that comes within the notice of pleasantly influenced wearers; but the same events and surroundings seen through frames fitted with ordinary Brazilian pebbles, assume a considerably harder colouring. My own honest summing up of Punchestown may be set down as follows: The weather was atrociously bad, in fact sufficiently so to wreck any festival in the world; the keenest of wintry winds blew over the course, and falls of snow were so frequent that umbrellas and waterproofs reigned supreme. At intervals, indeed, some adventurous fair ones displayed their fineries in places other than the stands, but on the whole the ladies had anything but a good time of it, and it was pitiable to watch some who had been full of faith when leaving town in the morning, going about in the afternoon with dainty footgear, soiled and smirched with melted snow and mud, and costly skirts draggled hopelessly to the knees. As for the wonders of the millinery displayed on the occasion, Boreas and Pluvius fought for it in approved style, and wrought untold ruin by their squabblings. The concourse in the fashionable sections of the ground was certainly stupendously large, but the general attendance did not at all average the assemblages of some former years. Of the boasted "improvements" made, I cannot speak in glowing language, because in all my experience of the place I never saw a greater confusion at "the gap," or more determined vehicular "push" at it, or indeed a greater number of narrow shaves from

H.R.H. THE DUKE OF YORK AND THE LORD-LIEUTENANT LEAVING THE VICE-REGAL LODGE.

FARMERS' CHALLENGE CUP—THE SINGLE.

IRISH GRAND MILITARY—THE WALL.

FARMERS' RACE—FIRST TIME ROUND.

NATIONAL HUNT CUP.

Dust and the Ladies' Hats

When the weather was fine dust invariably presented a problem, especially during the drive from Naas to the racecourse. Maybe the silk hat did not suffer so much from the dust as from the rain "although a combination of both was an unspeakable calamity", according to the reporter from the *Kildare Observer* writing about the April meeting in 1900.

"The ladies' hats, many of which were undoubtedly, masterpieces, might have suffered severely hadn't their fair wearers been forewarned and forearmed", he continued.

"Many a delicate creation of the milliner's art travelled the road to dusty Punchestown enveloped in white silk covers, that looked like turbans, and gave quite an Oriental appearance to the wearers".

"Enterprising gentlemen wait in ambush at the end of the drive and, armed with a clothes brush and an undeniable manner, fall upon the dusty fares. They did a flourishing trade. This brush with the enemy, as it might fairly be called, was in many cases unnecessary, for ample accommodation was provided by the courteous stewards for those who were under their care".

In fact, despite the absence of many of the military men from the Curragh and Newbridge and Naas, who were fighting in the Boer War, the two-day meeting was considered to be highly successful.

Another Special Occasion

Undoubtedly, the previous year, when the Duke and Duchess of York attended, was regarded as an exceptional one, but in 1900 the presence once again of Royalty made it another special occasion for many of the patrons of the Turf.

The Princess Henry of Battenburg, Princess Christian of Schleswig-Holstein, and the Duke of Connaught were there in the party of the Lord Lieutenant and Countess Cadogan, "with their respective suites". The red carpet was again laid out for the visitors whose arrival was greeted with cheers. It was noticed "that the scarlet uniform of the Royal servants added a pleasant gleam of colour to the scene". The Duke, who was Commander of the Forces in Ireland, and the two Princesses, were children of Queen Victoria.

HOW THE ILLUSTRATED SPORTING AND DRAMATIC NEWS... saw the Punchestown Meeting of 1899.

KILDARE AND NATIONAL HUNT AT PUNCHESTOWN

ARRIVAL OF SOME OF THE VICE-REGAL PARTY.

serious accident. The committee have erected stone piers on either side of the exit, but these are harder things to get one's legs crushed against than are old wooden posts or mud and bramble surroundings, and there still seems to be no possibility of more than one car passing out at a time, in anything resembling safety. Every John wants to be first, in order to get back and pick up more fares for conveyal to Naas Station; and with no kind of enforced order, or indeed, *chance* of enforcing or securing such, something of the dire confusion which prevailed may very well be imagined. Oh, the language! and the whipcord, and the dread in which the poor jaded horses must stand of the Madonna and Saints! Everything, however, seems to be fair at Punchestown, except the weather, when it resembles that of Tuesday and Wednesday; but I only hope that the poor hurt man who was crawling on his hands and knees like a Dervish, and who said he was looking out for a place to die, succeeded in finding one to his satisfaction!

I heard great grumbling among Pressmen about the lack of facilities for doing their reports, and the unfairness of granting them tickets for the general enclosure only: a place of all others to which legitimate sporting business would never take them. It seems incomprehensible how gentlemen so intelligent and painstaking as the Kildare Hunt executive can be so absolutely oblivious of the actual necessities of genuine Press workers. I thought, until an hour ago, that the uttering of a complaint would, as usual, be left to me to do; but a man has just informed me that the *Irish Times* in its reports of the meeting came down with quite legitimate heaviness upon the difficulties endured by Press-writers on the occasion of it. No doubt a uniformly courteous committee will need no further reminding of needed change; but it certainly ought to be kept well in view that representatives of important newspapers ought to be furnished with passes which will admit them to all departments in which they have legitimate business to transact.

In the matter of hospitality I never witnessed at any race meeting **a** more lavish display. The members of the hunt, the United Service Club men, the various regiments in garrison, and numerous other "associations" gave quite magnificent feasts, while owners of drags and carriages dispensed refreshments with generosity the most unbounded.

CONYNGHAM CUP—THE DOUBLE.

CONYNGHAM CUP—SECOND TIME ROUND, THE WALL.

NATIONAL HUNT CUP—THE DROP.

IRISH GRAND MILITARY—THE FIRST JUMP.

Silk Hats Compulsory!

The status of the Punchestown meeting in the annual social calendar was reflected in the amount of space devoted to the reports of the races themselves in the national and provincial press, and even down to the descriptions of the ladies' dresses. A column was filled with a list of the house parties arranged for the occasion. Then there followed a long list of ladies and gentlemen who attended the races, starting with the Earl of Clonmell and including numerous titled and military people.

An indication of the importance of military etiquette on such important occasions as Punchestown was given in the dress regulations issued to officers for attendances at the races. It was stipulated that on the first day silk hats were to be worn, but on the second day the ordinary felt hat would do.

Punchestown was recognised as one of the main events in the Irish social calendar, and the house parties in Dublin, Kildare and neighbouring counties were reported in detail in the newspaper. Hosting parties in 1900 were: the Earl of Mayo at Palmerstown, Sir Kildare Borrowes at Barretstown Castle, Sir Gerald Dease at Celbridge Abbey, Mr T.J. de Burgh at Oldtown, Mr D. More O'Ferrall at Kildangan, Mr A. Aylmer at Rathmore, Major Claude Cane at St.Wolstan's ,

Farmleigh as it looks today.

Capt. Hall at Prospect, Sir George Fitzgerald at Killibegs, Mr Percy La Touche at Harristown, Col. the Hon C.Crichton at Mullaboden and at the end of the list: Piercetown House, Newbridge, the home of the auctioneer R. J. Goff and Abbeylands, Naas, the home of J. Whiteside Dane, Clerk of the Crown & Peace, Co. Kildare.

Irish Grand Military - The Wall. Illustrated Sporting and Dramatic News 1899.

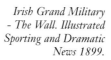

FIRST DAY

KILDARE AND NATIONAL HUNT

RACES

PUNCHESTOWN

TUESDAY AND WEDNESDAY,
APRIL 22nd & 23rd, 1913.

SPECIAL TRAINS.
Leave Kingsbridge for Naas at 10-20, 10-45,
and 11-25.
Returning from Naas 5-15 to 7 p.m.

Price Sixpence

The card for the first day in 1913, the year before the First World War broke out. It cost 6d (old money).

Derick Barton of Straffan in his *Memoirs* recalled when the house was full of guests for the meeting: "What this meant for the staff just beggars imagining. There were five double rooms with a dressing room for each, two further single rooms for lady guests and two single rooms for bachelors on the ground floor. This accounts for ten (stet) visitors (with the possibility of several extra on the attic floor). Quite obviously baths and bath water had to be provided in the bedrooms. It just does not bear thinking about".

Farmers Challenge Cup - The Single. Illustrated Sporting and Dramatic News 1899.

All the arrangements for the Royal visit to the 1900 meeting went well and it was the opinion of the racegoers that "a better day's sport than Tuesday has seldom been witnessed at Punchestown, despite hard going in the plough and clouds of dust!, And that despite the fact that two of the military races had to be cancelled, due to the lack of entries caused by the absence of officers away in the war.

A Literary Collection

Punchestown House was the country seat of Oxford graduate Thomas Tickell close friend of Joseph Addison of "Spectator" fame. His town residence in Glasnevin, where he and his wife Clotilda (daughter of Sir Maurice Eustace of Harristown) lived was close to "Delville" the home of Dr. and Mrs. Delaney, Dean Swift's friend. The 'Tickell Cup' was presented to Punchestown by another Tickell, Lt. Col. Edward James Tickell (a keen sportsman and a participant in the Olympic Games of 1912) Cup which was to be competed for by local riders.

"Princely Punchestown was again lacking in the usual splash of colour, so much part of the scene in later years, because of the death of Queen Victoria, but nevertheless it drew the crowds and maintained a certain festive air", wrote one observer in 1901. It had been expected that the Prince of Wales would again have attended the meeting, but of course that was not possible, nor could the Lord Lieutenant and his entourage be present. For the ladies who "graced the stands and course, black, with a mixture of white, was the prevailing colour, and hence there was an absence of that brilliancy of dress which is ever associated with this gathering".

General views of Punchestown during the 1896 meeting, eight years prior to the Prince of Wales returning to the course as King Edward VII.

1904 - The Court House, Naas bedecked with bunting and flags to celebrate the Royal Visit.

Dust Fog Prevailed

However, over a thousand racegoers came to Naas by train, "with one regular unbroken string of cars plying between Naas and the course for several hours previous to 1p.m. and a dust fog prevailed through the route. It was even worse on the return journey, when the traffic was somewhat speedier, which had the result of enveloping each car in a cloud of dust, making it impossible for the occupants of any vehicle to see those on another a dozen yards in font.

"The local authorities were mindful of the comfort of the people while in the town by having the streets well watered at a convenient hour previous to the traffic beginning, but provision might have been made for subjecting the streets to a similar process prior to the return of the evening traffic".

That the fame of the April meeting had spread across the Atlantic was proven by the publication of a long poem written by a lady from North Kildare in the *New York World*. It told the story of a horse named *Finn McCool* that had been purchased at the fair of Naas "and never an uglier object was seen", and which the owner believed "would make or break me at the races at Punchestown".

King Edward VII Attends

In 1904 the two-day meeting saw Edward VII and Queen Alexandra attend for both days, April 26th and April 27th and the attendance at the races that year was the biggest since 1868 when the King, as Prince of Wales, made his first visit.

The Royal party travelled from Kingsbridge Station in Dublin to Naas by special train and the loyal town fathers ensured that the County Town was *en fête* for the passage of the entourage through the main streets. The streets bedecked with Union Jacks, bunting and garlands of flowers, some arranged by Switzers of Dublin in regal style with crown-shaped pyramids or the lion and unicorn.

The Protestant and Catholic clergy combined with the local gentry and the town worthies in the preparations which were summarised by the Chairman of the reception committee, Mr William Staples, who said "Naas of the Kings should be making ready to welcome its King".

Mr Percy la Touche asked the Urban Council to have the streets sprayed with water to keep down the dust and over 300 members of the R.I.C. were drafted in to keep the peace.

There is little doubt that the King from his days in the Curragh as Prince of Wales had forged a special affinity with Punchestown and was very popular.

Conyngham Cup. Illustrated Sporting and Dramatic News 1899

But soon Royal visits would become more difficult, if not impossible. The introduction of the Home Rule Bill in the House of Commons in April 1912 proved an indication that the scene was changing swiftly and dramatically. The spirit of the day was reflected in a cartoon which was published in the *Irish Life* Supplement of April 17th, 1912. It depicted George V, the Kaiser and Lloyd George boarding the train to Sallins under the caption OFF TO PUNCHESTOWN!!!

Little Enthusiasm

When the Lord Lieutenant and his party drove in procession through the Punchestown course on April 23rd there was little enthusiasm from the crowds.

However, the house parties continued at Harristown, Straffan and the other hospitable houses in Kildare and adjoining counties. The journalist from *Irish Life* predicted a good attendance and fine weather "fair frocks, and there are few of us who fail to like the ladies at their best. But whatever the weather, it is one of the most notable features of Punchestown that the ladies never desert it, even if waterproofs and galoshes be the order of the going. Can one urge anything stronger for the enormous popularity of Glorious Punchestown?"

OFF TO PUNCHESTOWN!

Festival Time In Naas

The Punchestown meeting meant that it was festival time in Naas and in the old days the town benefited greatly from the influx of visitors, many of whom came by the special trains and stayed overnight.

Hackney cars did a roaring trade, the public houses were packed and the numerous itinerant vendors and trick men, who were annual visitors, added to the colour of the festival.

An Eye-Witness Account

Maurice Lendrum from Naas recalled those days: "When motor cars were unknown, and horse-drawn vehicles were the only means of transport, the better off provided themselves with relief horses for the journey from Dublin, stabling them at Rathcoole the night before".

"The streets of Naas were thronged with outside cars and cabs from every part of Ireland and the flotsam and jetsam of Dublin travellers in their wake, including musicians, hawkers, trick of the loop men and card manipulators.

All were making a harvest of the races, but no one was very particular about how the result was to be achieved. Every farmyard within three or four miles of Punchestown became the abode of a strange assortment of mendicants. They came from everywhere, and had their own pitches at the entrance to the course. One entrance is still known as Beggar's End where the down-and-out assembled.

"As there was then only one entrance to the racecourse there was a stampede as every vehicle jockeyed for position. It was a case of the survival of the fittest, with the Dublin jarvies edging everyone out as far as they could"

An old resident of Main Street, Naas had happy memories of observing as a child the excitement in the town on race day 1913. "Special trains arrived at the station, hackney cars did a roaring trade, each taking five passengers to the racecourse and returning at a gallop to pick up another load.

A motley assortment travelled on the hacks, well-dressed city men and ladies, professional types, officers and high-ranking government officials, sitting on a side-car with perhaps a dealer or even a 'three card' man, all with the one object in view, a day of pleasure and, perhaps, some profit, at Punchestown".

"My greatest memory of that race day in 1913 was the passing of the Lord Lieutenant's suite, preceded by a guard of military, the Lancers in gorgeous blue and gold uniforms, beautifully mounted, harness glistening in the sun, horses' coats groomed to perfection, and the pennants on the lances fluttering in the wind, a truly grand sight.

Naas en fete for the Passage of King Edward VII's entourage through the town on the way to Punchestown Races in 1904. Every building had its bunting, garlands and flowers and the Union Jack displayed proudly.

"The Lord Lieutenant was in an open coach, drawn by four magnificent blacks. He sat in the back seat, with a lady, while another lady and gentleman sat opposite. The men wore morning coats and top hats and looked very impressive to a small boy. The coachman and footmen occupied the front seat while, behind, another footman was stationed with a long trumpet which he blew every few hundred yards, When the Vice-Regal party had passed, the traffic slowly petered out, and a strange silence descended on Naas until the crowds returned after the last race".

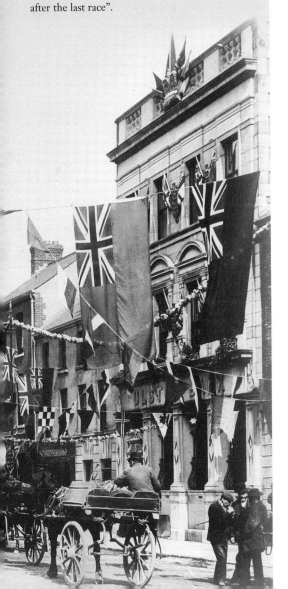

War takes its toll - but races went ahead in 1916

The outbreak of the First World War in 1914 had a dramatic effect on the Punchestown meeting and, indeed, those effects would be felt until hostilities finally ended on mainland Europe.

The involvement of the military sportsmen was the most noticeable and immediate repercussion. And as the officers stationed in Ireland went off to the front, much of the glamour they brought to the military races went with them.

But, amazingly enough, the 1916 Rebellion did not prevent Punchestown going ahead. It was not expected that the attendance would be large, "but it proved to be satisfactory enough; needless to remark, there was an absence of that gaiety and brightness which we were accustomed to in pre-War times and the Hunt Stand bore a particularly empty look.

"Khaki was strongly in evidence, and how thoroughly keen are the soldier sportsmen in assisting at the great chasing carnival was manifested by the large number of officers who spent a portion of their brief respite from trench work at the meeting. They included several capable horsemen".

The General Strike on April 23rd, 1918, called by the Irish Congress of Trade Unions as part of the resistance against the extension to Ireland of military conscription, coincided with the first day of the Punchestown Festival meeting that same year.

Although, according to the Irish Field, there was "total dislocation of business throughout the country for a whole day", the "great Kildare steeplechasing carnival" still managed to go ahead, though thousands missed out on it as a result of the suspension of rail services.

Many racegoers, determined not to miss out, wisely caught the last trains on the previous evening and the invasion of Naas and other towns in Kildare put a "severe strain on all available accommodation", according to one observer. Nevertheless the people of Naas and Sallins rose to the occasion in style.

While fierce fighting waged in the battle-fields of the First World War, the Kildare Hunt Cup and the Conyngham were being battled for as usual over the famous banks and ditches.

Political Scene Changing

But with a changing political scene, Sinn Fein began to disrupt meetings of the Hunt, causing it to be temporarily suspended. The reaction of the Hunt Club was a proposal to abandon the April Races and the concerned farmers called a meeting in Naas which was attended by between four and five hundred people.

There a list of 1,500 farmers was displayed, all requesting that hunting should be continued and the races held. The loss of business to horse breeders, to farming in general and to the local traders was feared.

However, the races were abandoned that year (1919) and the loss of business not alone in the County of Kildare itself but in Dublin was expressed in the newspapers. Hotels and boarding houses were closed, the jarveys idle and there was none of the traditional decorating of houses in the Naas district.

The business people of the county were forcefully made aware that the boom days of the War were gone and a different world was being created.

As the War for Independence intensified on the domestic front, the meeting of 1920 was abandoned. In 1920 a General Strike was again called, this time in sympathy with Republican prisoners who had gone on hunger strike in Mountjoy. It happened that April 13th was the opening day of the Punchestown Festival meeting. So badly was public transport hit that the meeting was first postponed and then cancelled.

A shadow hung over the 1921 meeting as well and there were grave doubts whether it would go ahead. In his diary Mark Sturgis, a senior official in Dublin Castle wrote: "All racing stopped in England, I believe. Will Punchestown come off next week?"

But it was found possible to go ahead with the 1921 meeting after all and it was judged to have been particularly successful. Sturgis attended both days, after he had first made early visits to Dublin Castle. "Tuesday was like June, and we couldn't go wrong. Rachel netted £50. I had a talk to Parkinson (a veterinary surgeon and a leading trainer and racehorse owner of Maddenstown Lodge, the Curragh. He was appointed to the Seanad in 1922) in the paddock".

During the 1922 meeting two armed men held up the driver and stole the Crossley Salon of the Lord Lieutenant.

Nevertheless the gaiety was not too suppressed and that year for the first time Mrs Bridget Lawlor catered for the Hunt Ball, which was held as usual in Naas Town Hall. Two decades later Mrs Lawlor, who was then celebrated for her catering at the meeting, was described as "a Punchestown heroine if ever there was one, for she was born on the spot and the races still go over part of her brother's land".

"A Truly Irish Atmosphere"

The year 1923 marked a historic landmark in the chequered history of Punchestown. "It was the first meeting held in a truly Irish atmosphere with not even the Lord Lieutenant to pay a visit official or unofficial", wrote the correspondent of the *Leinster Leader*. And the *Kildare Observer*, under the heading "Good Omen" observed that "what was formerly the State visit of the Viceregal Party to the races was this year marked by the appearance of the Governor-General, Mr T.M. (Tim) Healy, President W.T. Cosgrove and other members of the Cabinet.

"They passed through Naas on their way to the course without any display such as was associated with the visit of the Lord Lieutenant in the old days, and few knew of their visit until they were met at the Grand Stand by several of the Stewards.

But the presence of the Governor-General was not without drama. Local lore is that as, for the first time, the Union Jack was not being raised, it was intended by the hunt committee not to fly any flag. But the new government insisted that the Tricolour should be raised before the official party arrived, and there was a flurry to get a flag pole erected at the last minute.

"The Governor-General made his first bet on Mr. Harry Beasley's mount, Pride of Arras and it may be regarded as an auspicious fact for the Free State that His Excellence backed a winner. Rumours of attempts at interference with the meeting, or with visitors travelling by road or rail, proved without foundation, no doubt due to the military activity and precautions taken prior to and during he races".

Two hundred Civic Guards were drafted in for the races, and their task of regulating the traffic through Naas was made more difficult by "the Dublin jarvies' inclination to regulate the traffic to suit themselves". The Guards also made a swoop on the vendors "who supplemented their non-excisable commodities by large supplies of stout, and some 70 dozen of stout was seized, a severe penalty for the enterprise of the dealers, who have not, of course, heard the last of the offence".

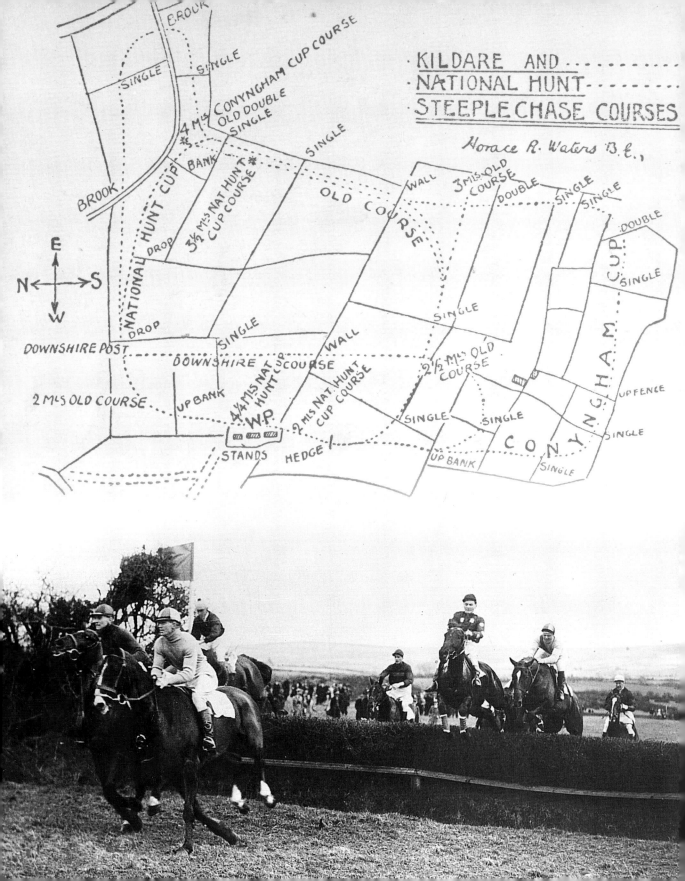

KILDARE AND
NATIONAL HUNT
STEEPLE CHASE COURSES

Horace R. Waters B.E.,

3

PESSIMISTIC FORECASTS
PROVED WRONG
PUNCHESTOWN 1925
AN UNSURPASSED OCCASION

Round about 1925 some questions were being asked on the merits of the Punchestown meeting and undoubtedly some of these arose from the fact that three riders had been killed on the course over a number of years.

"Some veteran patrons of the course were beginning to presume that the greatness of the steeplechase was in decline", wrote one commentator. And he went on… "I have seen some of the best steeplechase horses in the world run on this track. Perhaps we will never see their like again for pluck and stamina. There are few chasers at the present time that would show any form or even get around this Punchestown country and I am afraid getting fewer, as they do not seem to have the bone, the muscle or wear and tear about them for such a severe test."

Design (H.J. Delmage) triumphs in the Punchestown Cup in 1934.

Kildare and National Hunt Steeplechase Courses 1908.

Another commentator made the point that it was "the fashion to assert that Punchestown is but a shadow of its former grandeur since the British Army left. They, with their lavish hospitality, are indeed sadly missed by the old brigade."

Unsurpassed Renewal of '25

While it seemed to have become the fashion with some critics to say that Punchestown was but a shadow of its former grandeur since the British Army left, the old brigade, in particular, missing their lavish hospitality, it cannot be denied that the renewal of 1925 was unsurpassed by any of its predecessors. And that was the recorded opinion of writers whose memories of the great April meeting went back a long time.

Certainly the crowd was never larger. Officers of the Free State Army did their best to fill the void left by the departure of the British Army.

They attended in uniform for the first time in peace time and had their own luncheon and tea-rooms, where lavish hospitality was dispensed in keeping with the tradition of the old days.

In 1925 the distinguished soldier and local resident, General Sir Bryan Mahon, King's Royal Irish Hussars, Senior Steward of the Irish Turf Club and former Senior Steward of the Irish National Hunt Steeplechase, was appointed Manager of Punchestown.

Yet, all the pessimistic viewpoints were proved wrong in the end. The 1925 meeting was, according to general consensus, unsurpassed by any of its predecessors. Indeed this was the recorded opinion of writers whose memories of the great April meeting went back a long time.

Around this time some questions arose about the merits of the fixture and whether there were now the horses in the country able to cope with the singular and unique challenge that Punchestown presented.

Gen. Sir Bryan Mahon, Manager of Punchestown in 1925

Three Riders Killed

Three riders had been killed on the course over a number of years. In 1892, Willie Beasley suffered fatal injuries in a fall at the "Herds Garden" Bank on April 27th from which he never fully recovered consciousness. He died on May 9th.

The horse he was riding was named All is Well. Before the race a friend of the family Mrs W.P. Cullen, unsuccessfully begged Willie not to ride as she had a dream of a fatal accident which proved actually correct in every detail. She withdrew her own intended runner which he was due to ride but he went and got the mount on All is Well.

The Big Double claimed a jockey named O'Donnell in 1914 and about 1930 Tony Drum was the victim of another fatal fall.

W. T. Cosgrave, as leader of the Irish Free State, proved himself extremely supportive of Irish and breeding interests throughout the difficult twenties and integrated the old ascendancy into the new order of things to ensure a smooth transition. His son Liam T. Cosgrave, Taoiseach from 1973-77, involved all his life in racing, opened the new Turf Club headquarters on the Curragh in December, 1976. He is still a regular attender at the races, Leopardstown particularly.

MAY

Sun.	1	8	15	22	29
Mon.	2	9	16	23	30
Tu.	3	10	17	24	31
Wed.	4	11	18	25	
Th.	5	12	19	26	
Fri.	6	13	20	27	
Sat.	7	14	21	28	

DAILY SKETCH

THURSDAY, MAY 5, 1927.   Head Office: 200, Gray's Inn-road, W.C.1.   'Phone: Museum 9841.

Save 50, but fill in three top coupons only
"DAILY SKETCH" CHILDREN'S BIRTHDAY CLUB
OUR MAGIC BADGE A FREE "SEASON TICKET"
FOR NEARLY 200 ATTRACTIONS

NAME

ADDRESS

Print your name, address, etc., clearly in block letters

IRISH SPORT LOVERS AT PUNCHESTOWN RACES

Lord and Lady Ossory at the Kildare and National Hunt race meeting at Punchestown.—(*Daily Sketch.*)

Left: Baron De Robeck.   Right : Mr. and Mrs. Kevin O'Higgins.—(*Daily Sketch.*)

Mrs. J. W. Osborne leading in her husband's victorious Alice Whitethorn, winner of the Kildare Hunt Cup.—(*Daily Sketch.*)

Lord Fitzwilliam (in grey coat) watching the racing at Punchestown.—(*Daily Sketch.*)

Lady Weldon (left) and Lord Castlemaine were among prominent Irish sportsmen and sportswomen on the members' stand.—(*Daily Sketch.*)

Governor-General T. Healy surveying the handsome trophies which Major-General McKeon is showing to Lady Ossory.—(*Daily Sketch.*)

Another peep at the members' stand. The races attracted a big throng of Irish sport lovers.—(*Daily Sketch.*)

Even if fewer top hats were worn at the second day of the meeting in 1928 and the political element was less prominent, owing to the assembly of the Dail, than on the first day, an English visitor found the meeting, "at once soothing and exhilarating, and I am going to advise my friends in London to come along and enjoy themselves in the right way".

The first day of the races that year was described graphically in the *Irish Times* as "a brilliant race meeting, reminiscent of the Old Times... a little green plain, with hummocks here and there, set in an amphitheatre of white-capped hills, golden gorse and greening trees, cumulous clouds moving across a clear blue sky, a great concourse of happy, gossiping people, merriment and gaiety, horses exercising, the loud shouts of bookmakers, Punchestown yesterday. My friend was right, there is nothing quite like Peerless Punchestown anywhere that I know. It is remote from big centres of population but mid-April always sees a great gathering there.

A note was inserted on the front cover of the race card for the 1929 meeting requesting ladies not to wear native fox furs.

How the Daily Sketch *captured the Meeting of 1927.*

"Yesterday's gathering was characteristic of the famous meeting. Retired British Generals rubbed shoulders with officers of the young Free State Army, members of the nobility chatted in friendly fashion with Free State Ministers and Dail Deputies, foreign Consuls had a flutter like ordinary mortals. It was, in short, a great social gathering where the horse was almost the sole topic of conversation".

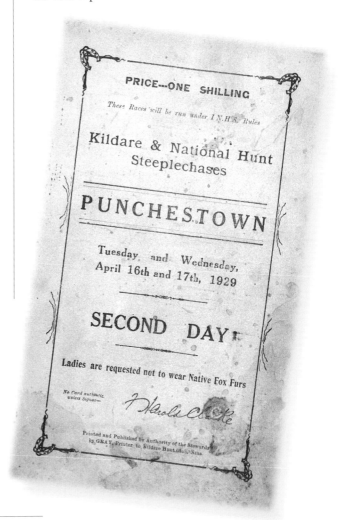

PRICE---ONE SHILLING

These Races will be run under I.N.H.S. Rules

Kildare & National Hunt Steeplechases

PUNCHESTOWN

Tuesday and Wednesday, April 16th and 17th, 1929

SECOND DAY.

Ladies are requested not to wear Native Fox Furs

Printed and Published by Authority of the Stewards by GRAY, Printer to Kildare Hunt Club, Naas.

NCHESTOWN CARNIVAL

DONOHILL WINNING THE BIG CUP

REVEALS PLAN

Fame Pursued Him At Punchestown Yesterday

Mr. Fred Astaire (centre) at Punchestown yesterday.—*Irish Independent* photo (P.C.).

FILM STAR WAS KEPT BUSY

"Irish Independent" Woman Reporter.

MR. FRED ASTAIRE, dance star of the films, went racing at Punchestown yesterday and the moment he was seen, women visitors forgot their own and other women's clothes, horses and betting. They looked for his small, tweed-clad figure, gave him their autograph books and racing cards to sign and tried to exchange a word with him.

He was the most patient, pleasant-mannered, and good-humoured visitor the course nearly spoilt his admirers yesterday, and he took it all in good autograph

Fred Astaire, dance star of the films, pictured at Punchestown '39. Other famous personalties who also went racing at Punchestown included Bing Crosby and Jack Doyle, known as the 'Gorgeous Gael' in his prime as a boxer.

Back on the Map

Derick Barton, married and settled at Straffan since 1927, was aware that Naas Town Hall was no longer a popular venue for the Hunt Ball, with numbers shrinking each year. With his wife, he was determined to put the Kildare Hunt Ball back on the map and they offered their house at Straffan "and had three highly-successful Balls there. From one point of view also it was a happy event to have the old house come to life again and filled with people".

Percy Was There

Percy French, according to the well-known writer, the poet Stephen Rynne, made his first public appearance as an entertainer at Punchestown Races. He was an apprentice in the Midland Railway at the time and quite unknown. What a gay, irresponsible fellow he was with his blackened face and Dixie Minstrel act! Was he absorbing local colour for the rollicking verses of *Carmody's Mare*. Percy and Punchestown fitted one another like hand and glove.

His poetic version of the mythical instructions given by Queen Victoria to Lord Zetland had included this injunction:

Take a party down, sez she,
To Punchestown, sez she.

Following his father's death in 1927, Barton succeeded to the position his father had held with the Kildare Hunt Club.

Unfortunately, a long smouldering controversy was to develop between the Club and its offspring the Kildare Hunt Races (more generally known as 'Punchestown').

The Hunt Club's financial affairs were in a more than critical state and from time to time a rescue operation had to be carried out by Punchestown, whose controllers resented the fact that after each rescue the situation was quickly in crisis again.

Despite the hardship of the Economic War years in the Thirties, Punchestown still drew big crowds for its Spring Fesrival meeting. A general view of the field passing the stand in 1938.

Much ill-feeling was engendered between partisans on either side (broadly speaking the Hunting and the Racing elements). Among other things the Hunt Club held the appointment of a manager for Punchestown but, having appointed him they had no control over his actions-nor could they dismiss him. Tact and conciliation eventually achieved a modus vivendi which has worked down the years to a very sensible accommodation.

The New Ireland

Punchestown survived the Economic War of the Thirties, as did the Kildare Hunt. In 1933 a Ball was held as usual on the night of the second day's racing at Mrs Lawlor's new Ballroom in Naas.

The list of patrons reflected the New Ireland. There were no titled gentlemen or ladies and the only military listed were half a dozen officers from the Curragh Camp.

The field clearing the Stone Wall.

The majority of the revellers were professional and business people who paid 7/6 for a sit-down supper and music by *Peter Keogh's Band* which he "personally conducted".

The changed political scene, with *Fianna Fail* now in office, also brought new dignitaries to the meeting. Derick Barton was fulfilling his duty as Chairman of the Hunt in entertaining Mr De Valera, who remarked to him (apropos of the strife that was going on in Cyprus at the time between Greek and Turk): "You know, Mr Barton, civil war is the worst thing that can overtake a nation".

Making the best possible use of a gap in a hedge as interested spectators at right follow the progresses of the race.

The Kildare Hunt held its own Ball at Russborough where, *The Tatler* noted, "although since the departure of the Military the fields in Kildare are shrunken from their former plethoric state, the Hunt Ball at Russborough House produced no lack of enthusiasts".

The Emergency Years

During *The Emergency* (as the Second World War period became known in Ireland) racing continued at Punchestown - even though the meetings of 1941 and '43 had to be cancelled.

It was amazing in a way that only two years were lost when one reflects on the fact that strict petrol rationing was in operation, and on the austerity of those days.

One observer writing about the meeting of 1944 noted that "although the crowds were, needless to say, not as big as usual, there was a surprisingly large attendance in the circumstances, especially on the second afternoon".

He went on to describe "the fantastic variety of horse-drawn conveyances, not to mention bicycles and their derivation of every character imaginable. In fact, the horse played as much part in providing racgoers as it did races. Into service came brakes, jaunters, wagonettes, four-wheelers, traps and gigs of ever conceivable make and shape, farm carts and even the humble ass and cart. Believe me or not, one gallant and obviously determined gentleman arrived in a bath-chair".

"The farm cart, especially the smooth-running type, fitted with what were called balloon-type wheels, was quite a popular mode of transport, and not a few house parties, ladies in the Punchestown modes, and their smartly groomed escorts, made the journey in such a vehicle seated in comfort in well-upholstered chairs. Many true Punchestown devotees who cycled to the course had put at least thirty miles behind them, for it was considered a well worthwhile pedal in those days of austerity".

During The Emergency (Second World War period) racing had to be cancelled in 1941 and 1943 but the meeting of 1944 went ahead and here Kilgowan is pictured winning the Sallins Plate.

"Needless to say, transport did not deter the itinerant class either; austerity is something they live with, and the whine of the beggar was heard in the land, a minor accompaniment to the stentorian voices of gentlemen who lay the odds".

Mrs Lawlor, the caterer for the meetings, did not have a transport problem as she travelled to the racecourse in her small phaeton, while her staff arrived on drays. And some of the internees from the Curragh Camp also managed to enjoy the festival, availing of the leniency of their military minders.

Home from a POW Camp

The affection which Kildare people had for the meeting was typified in the delight expressed by Major Charles Marcus Lefevre Clements of Killadoon, Celbridge when he returned home from a POW camp in Germany in 1945 "happy to be just in time for the Punchestown Races". As a long-standing and enthusiastic member of the Kildare Hunt Club it was a very special meeting for him as he met old friends, many of whom had also been in the War.

But Punchestown held its own in the War years, despite travel restrictions and other privations.

The year 1946 opened a new chapter in its history. A chronicler of the time put it picturesquely: "The premier Hunt Carnival, admitting of no superior in racing of its type, is dear to the hearts of every sporting son and daughter of our verdant isle. Ireland is a nation of horse lovers, and though its children may be deeply interested in Flat racing, it is the thrill of chasing which is nearest to their hearts".

Snow forces Postponement

The celebration of the 100th anniversary of the Punchestown meeting in 1950 was unfortunately severely curtailed. As the *Leinster Leader* reported, snow caused the postponement of the first day card. "The thousands of racegoers who attended on the Tuesday found little to enthuse about in the snow-blanketed picturesque scene, as shivering in Arctic conditions they listened to the official announcement of the decision to postpone".

On the Wednesday, it was observed, that "the lure of Punchestown remains as strong as ever, no matter what the difficulties encountered... overlooking the moving masses from the height of the stands, one was almost awed by the immensity of the crowd. It can be said, without fear of contradiction, that every nationality was represented there".

Mary Byrne from Naas, who was also there that day, was able to boast that she had been attending Punchestown for 75 years and seldom missed a meeting.

SIBERIAN CONDITIONS... graphically captured in this picture is the snowstorm that caused racing to be postponed for a day - April 29th - in 1950, the year that saw the celebration of the Centenary of Punchestown.

Moves to Modernise

During the Centenary Year of 1950 moves were made in favour of modernising Punchestown, but the *Leinster Leader* disagreed, holding that Punchestown "as it is today represented the best of all-round tests of a jumper and that means a lot in the world. Modernise Punchestown and you will to a great extent change all that. You may have a shinier, sleeker, more prosperous venue, but gone forever will be the meaning of Punchestown, which is not just another race meeting, but a meeting with a difference, over a course which can be described as a law unto itself".

And Punchestown continued to prosper and to retain its immense popularity with the people, perhaps typified in the person of the Dunlavin punter, James Lawlor who could, in 1963, boast that he had never missed a meeting in eighty years! Journalist Mary Norton (*Monica Carr*) nostalgically recalled in April 1992 that "at this time of the year Punchestown which was, in this neck of the woods, only second to Christmas in the Thirties, Forties and Fifties, the very idea of attending in comfortable clothes, gloveless, hatless and flat-heeled, was something we never contemplated. You dressed up 'for the Races' as you did for Mass on Sunday, suffering headaches from unaccustomed pressure of hats, something you accepted uncomplainingly".

Walking Sunday

The Tradition of "Walking Sunday" goes back a long time and that is how the Sunday before the Festival meeting is known in County Kildare. For County Kildare people, and in particular the people of Naas, Walking Sunday, was an integral part of the scene - an annual ritual - in the lead-up to the great Spring meeting. It was customary for the townsfolk of Naas to walk out to Punchestown to join the crowds on the racecourse and there to inspect the jumps and predict the going for the races. For the children all the fun of the fair was on the outside, with the swing boats, the fruit stalls and ice-cream waggons.

Shop fronts and houses in the town of Naas were painted "for Punchestown", as were those on the roads to the racecourse. The schools, banks and shops closed to enable everyone to attend the races, thus uniting the farming, racing and hunting folk with the business world and the thousands of enthusiasts for whom Punchestown was also the principal holiday of the year.

One lady remembers from the days of The Emergency the selection of sweets on the stalls set up for the day by sellers from various parts. The Naas Athletic Club's three-mile race for the Millbrook Cup - a cross country handicap race - became part of the day from around 1926.

Of the county families which were founder-members of the Punchestown meeting only the de Burghs and their cousins, the de Robecks maintained their continuous interest in the organisation and management of the steeplechase until recent years being, at different times, Chairmen of the Punchestown Committee.

Punchestown a Stage

As the perceptive writer Stephen Rynne commented thirty-five years ago: "The races of Punchestown make a stage where all the players are stage Irishmen. The toffs on the stands, the tinkers on the field, the farmers in their glad-rags, the picnicing parties of the city folk, three-card trick men, trick-o'-the-loop men, pickpockets and by no means last (as they say) the jockeys. What a magnificent, all-star cast".

More recently the Naas poet Timmy Conway commenced his poem *Sights and Sounds of Punchestown* with the verse:

> *The calendar of my youth read:*
> *In the beginning there was Christmas*
> *Then there was Easter*
> *And then there was Punchestown.*
> *The priest from the altar*
> *"To-day is Walking Sunday*
> *This is the fifth Sunday after Easter*
> *This is the first Sunday before Punchestown".*

Another graphic shot on the day racing was postponed in 1950 showing bookies "folding their tents", in the midst of the snowstorm.

Air Corps photograph of Punchestown Racecourse
during the 1950's

4

PRINCE OF WALES DRAWS
AN IMMENSE CROWD OF 150,000

Raymond Smith

In the long and chequered history of Punchestown Racecourse one event that dwarfs all others for the lasting impact it made was the visit of the Prince of Wales in 1868.

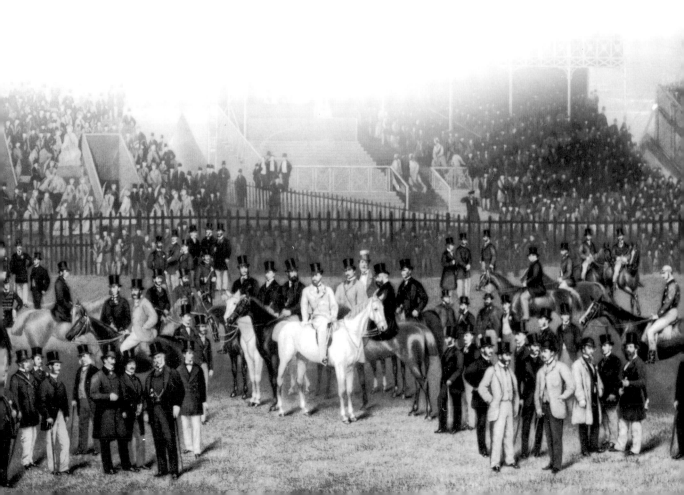

The attendance on the first day - Thursday, April 16 - was estimated at 150,000 and it is true to say that it set a global record that will possibly never be broken.

The Prince had a special feeling for Punchestown and identified closely with its special appeal from the time he was posted to the Curragh as a Colonel. The records of the period reveal that his dash on social occasions created more of an aura around his personality than anything he achieved as an officer.

HONOURING THE PRINCE OF WALES... among the renowned personalities of the period in the painting below were the Earl of Clonmell (on horse-back at extreme left), Captain Mc Calmont 7th Hussars, the Baron de Robeck (standing just to the right of the Prince), the Earl of Wicklow, Marquis of Drogheda, Marquis of Downshire, Sir Edward Kennedy, Mr. Thomas Connolly. Lord Otto Fitzgerald M.P., Viscount Doneraile, Prince Edward of Saxe Weimer is also in the group at right.

No Stranger

But even then he was no stranger to Ireland. In 1849 he had made his first visit to the country at the age of seven when he accompanied his parents. In 1858 he spent a short holiday in the South.

The Prince of Wales would pay a second visit to Punchestown in 1885, this time accompanied by the Princess and their eldest son Prince Albert Victor. And in 1904, he returned as King Edward VII with the Queen and their daughter, Princess Victoria, who went racing with him. His love of National Hunt racing and his special affection for Punchestown endeared him to the people.

It was fitting that before he departed the course, he should be presented with a race programme bound in purple leather, displaying a crimson and gold crown above an imprint of shamrock, rose and thistle treated in gold, green and crimson - an attempt to incorporate the King's racing colours in an artistic design.

Lasting Memento

That race programme in a way would stand as a lasting memento to the bonds he had forged with Punchestown over a span of more than forty years from the time he served in officer's uniform on the Curragh to the first decade of the twentieth century.

The status that the initial visit by the Prince of Wales gave to Punchestown was immeasurable. Thereafter, the Spring meeting would stand on a pedestal apart as a unique National Festival.

The Prince did not confine himself to attending on just one day in a perfunctory manner, as if it was demanded of him. No, he went on two successive days and entered totally into the spirit of the occasion.

King Edward VII arrives at the course for the Punchestown meeting of 1904 and would see Ambush II carrying his colours, contest the Prince of Wales's Plate. Ambush II had won at Punchestown in 1898 on his way to an epic victory in the 1900 Aintree Grand National, beating previous winner Manifesto.

On the second day, he remained on for the entire programme of five races. More important still, his Royal Highness, accompanied by several gentlemen of the Kildare Hunt, rode round the course after the Conyngham Cup and made a point of traversing the plain to see the field in a subsequent race cross the great Double Bank.

The Prince wrote from Dublin Castle to the Queen informing her of the "wonderfully enthusiastic reception" accorded him and his party by the Punchestown crowd, adding: "As I mentioned before, it gave an opportunity for all the country people to see us".

Their Duty

Forty-eight years before the 1916 Rising British Royalty saw it as part of their duty to visit their subjects in Ireland and give the populace a chance of displaying their "loyalty". Indeed, the Prince of Wales himself went on record to state that Punchestown would afford "a large concourse of people from all parts of the country, who look upon these races as a kind of annual National Festival, to have a better opportunity of seeing me than in Dublin".

He hinted that his principal reason for coming to Ireland was "on account of the Races", though he acknowledged to the Queen that it would not look good if that were stated to the public.

The Prince of Wales had the pleasure of seeing the inaugural running of the Prince of Wales's Plate (valued £500) on his first day at Punchestown.

Dust Rose in Clouds

Picture the scene as the thousands headed for the racecourse causing the roads to become a veritable sea of humanity. Adding to the fever and excitement was the fact that it was a glorious April day. And because of the dry weather, dust rose in clouds; men appeared suddenly to have turned old in a twinkling as their hair and beards - in the case of those sporting a beard - turned white. But nothing deterred the crowds, not even the swirling dust, from their determination to make it to the Races.

The Railway Company could not cope with the throngs who decided to go by rail. Every available piece of rolling stock at Kingsbridge (now Heuston station) was pressed into service and still there was no way that the overwhelming demand could be met.

Sat Upon

Passengers who found seats were themselves sat upon by others; and many who failed to get into a compartment climbed up on the roofs of the carriages where they lay holding on to one another - as the *Irish Times* put it "in a spirit of mutual confidence and brotherly affection". If there had been a tunnel between Kingsbridge and Inchicore as there was between Glanmire and Kilbarry, one can only contemplate with horror what would have become of those bestraddling the roofs of the carriages.

Picture the roads leading to Punchestown chock-a-block with the vehicles that were the popular mode of transport of that era - drawn by horses, mules, jennets and donkeys.

"Luckily, they could do little more than trot, so collisions, though frequent, were not apparently fatal", noted S.J. Watson in his book *Between The Flags*.

At Their Wit's End

Those responsible for the security of the Prince and Princess of Wales and the rest of the Royal party must have been at their wit's end as they contemplated the task of clearing the road between Sallins railway station and Punchestown (the Royal party had gone by rail in a special train from Kingsbridge). In the event, though their Royal Highnesses arrived an hour late at the racecourse, nothing untoward occurred *en route*. A contingent of 300 constabulary had been assembled at Naas. The authorities at Dublin Castle had taken a "calculated risk" in freeing political detainees in a gesture of goodwill and, even though official nerves were somewhat frayed after the murder "by person or persons unknown" of Mr. J.H. Fetherston Haugh, D.LO., J.P. near Kilcullen on April 15 1868, the visit of the Prince of Wales to Punchestown went off without incident, and was deemed, as already seen, as an outstanding success.

On the second day of the 1868 meeting timely April showers laid the fierce and unpleasant dust of the first day to rest. This time the attendance though still very large, did not come anyway near the record crowd of the previous day.

The Prince of Wales saw the redoubtable Mr. W. Trocke of the 35th (Sussex) Regiment win the principal event, the Conyngham Cup on Mr. Harper's mare, Olympia, beating twelve other contenders. On the first day, Mr. Trocke had won the Drogheda Stakes on Mr. G. Knox's Lysander. There were thirteen runners of which three fell.

Easing the Situation

Agrarian troubles, as the tenantry battled for a new deal and a better way of life through the activities of the Land League, had reared their head in the early 1880's. The number of 'incidents' which had numbered 4,439 in 1881 had fallen to 774 in 1884 but still the British Prime Minister, Mr. Gladstone and the Lord Lieutenant, Earl Spencer, thought, it would be a good move to prevail on the Queen, who was very reluctant it must be said, to send the Prince of Wales on another visit to Ireland in 1885, accompanied by the Princess and their eldest son. Political circles in London did not hide the fact that what was described as the "tact" of the Prince of Wales was being employed to "ease the political situation in Ireland". And no doubt not forgotten was the enthusiastic reception he had received at Punchestown Races in 1868.

The reception accorded the Royal party was reported to be cordial in Dublin, hostile in Mallow, dour in Cork and enthusiastic in Belfast.

On getting back from the South to Dublin, their Royal Highnesses went to Punchestown with the Lord Lieutenant and Lady Spencer on Tuesday, April 21st. They travelled by special train from Kingsbridge and, while the ordinary trains for the day stopped at Sallins, the Royal train, preceded by a pilot engine, went on down the recently opened branch line to a new station at Naas.

The glorious sunshine of the first day of the 1868 meeting was replaced on this occasion by heavy rain which began to fall as the Royal party arrived at Naas.

King Edward VII being greeted by Baron de Robeck and other dignitaries of the Punchestown Committee.

The steady downpour persisted throughout the afternoon and the *Irish Times* reported that it was a disaster for the ladies who had come out in all their finery and "beautiful bonnets or hats".

Lord Drogheda, a Steward of the Irish Turf Club, was there to welcome the Prince of Wales, as he had welcomed him on his first visit to Punchestown. But the intervening years had brought changes in personnel among the members of the Kildare Hunt Stewards. The new faces included Percy la Touche and A. More O'Ferrall, both of whom would in time become household names in Irish racing circles.

Also in the welcoming party was the young seventh Earl of Mayo whose father had escorted the Prince of Wales to view the Double-Bank in the Herd's Garden on April 17, 1868 (the sixth Earl of Mayo when Viceroy of India had been assassinated by a convict when visiting the penal settlement in the Andaman Islands on February 8, 1872).

Novel Approach

The Prince of Wales had the pleasure of seeing in action two of the famous Beasley brothers - Harry and Willie. Harry rode two winners during the afternoon and Willie one. He also witnessed an amazing race for the Kildare Hunt Cup. Nancy, owned by Baron de Robeck and ridden by his son Mr. H. de Robeck, slipped and fell at the first fence, but her rider remounted, caught up with the rest of the field at the Herd's Corner and went on to win easily. Then in the Conyngham Cup, Count Zboroweski's Billet Doux, winner of the Irish Grand National earlier that year, lost out to the outsider John Kane, owned by William Hanway, a County Kildare farmer, who also trained the horse himself.

His training methods were unique. It was his practice, according to S.J. Watson in *Between The Flags*, to let his racehorses loose in a big field and then set collie dogs after them to make them gallop. It was "a performance both horses and dogs enjoy so much that they get plenty of it". At all events, William Hanway's novel approach to training meant that his contenders "either won or got placed in the Farmers' Race at Punchestown for years".

Again, the Prince of Wales received a warm and friendly welcome - the "few insignificant hisses" that were heard in the vicinity of the Royal enclosure were promptly drowned out by loud cheers. Even then, late in the 19th. century, it was regarded as unbecoming and, indeed, rank bad form to introduce politics into a sporting occasion, especially a race meeting.

The Prince of Wales, because of a cold, did not make it to the second day of the 1885 Punchestown meeting and missed seeing Harry Beasley record a treble. But Prince Albert Victor, who was being treated then as the future King of England, was there with Lord Spencer, despite the continuing wet weather. So inclement was the weather, in fact, that even though Prince Albert Victor carefully studied the colours, he "could hardly recognise them when they came to weigh in, so mud-bespattered were the gay jackets".

Prince Albert Victor never made it to the throne of England, and never came back as King to a Punchestown meeting. He died from complications after influenza on January 14, 1892, when only 28.

Back as King

But the Prince of Wales would return to his favourite meeting as King and seemed to glory in every visit to the racecourse.

Queen Victoria, the "Great White Queen" had died on January 22, 1901 and only two European monarchs - King Louis XIV of France and the Emperor Francis Joseph of Austria - had reigned longer. In September of that year Lord Cadogan, the Viceroy, who had survived the Charge of the Heavy Brigade with the 4th Dragoons at Balaclava, drew up a programme for the visit to Ireland of King Edward V11, planned for the following Spring. As events turned out, the Royal visit was postponed until 1903 and it took place from July 21st to August 1st. It was the first time that any British King had come to Ireland accompanied by his Queen.

After reviewing 10,000 troops in the Phoenix Park, the King went racing at the new Park racecourse but did not get to Punchestown that year. However the King and Queen were back in Ireland in the Spring of 1904 and on the very morning of their arrival set out by train for Naas and the Punchestown Races, accompanied by their daughter, Princess Victoria. It was undoubtedly a day touched by nostalgia and many memories for the King as he reflected back on the crowd of 150,000 which had thronged the racecourse on the occasion of his first visit there as Prince of Wales in 1868. Deep down he was a lover of National Hunt racing more than the Flat and as in 1868, the weather again, was gloriously fine.

THEY WON IN FRONT OF THE PRINCE OF WALES...
PUNCHESTOWN WINNERS 1868... the line-up
of the horses and riders who triumphed on the occasion
of the historic visit of the Prince of Wales in 1868.
William Frocke rode both the winners of the Drogheda
Stakes and the Conyngham Cup.

The King's Runner

The crowd was immense - the biggest since 1868. A major attraction was the presence in the field for the Prince of Wales's Plate of Ambush 11, bearing the King's colours. This horse had been acquired for 500 guineas by King Edward when he was Prince of Wales and had won the Maiden Plate at Punchestown in 1898 on his way to victory in an epic battle for the 1900 Aintree Grand National, in which he beat the previous winner Manifesto (then a 12 year old carrying 12st. 13lbs.), who was eased by George Williamson when he saw that the contest was lost and so Barsac denied him runner-up position by a neck. "One of the most memorable Grand Nationals on record", was how *The Field* described it, adding that "those with the longest memories had to admit that they could recall nothing like it".

The Prince of Wales gave £500 to the winning rider, £250 to the Head Lad at Eyrefield Lodge on the Curragh where Ambush 11 was trained and £50 to the boy who 'did' the Royal horse. (Translate those presents into the money terms of today and you appreciate even more the scale of the future King's generosity in victory).

Ambush 11 did not contest the 1901 Aintree Grand National because of the appalling blizzard that swept the course. He was going best of all in the 1903 National when he took a crashing fall at the last fence and, despite his disappointment, the King's first concern was for the well-being of the rider. "I hope Anthony is not hurt", he remarked.

It was Algy Anthony who was in the saddle again at Punchestown on April 26 1904 but that fall in the Grand National of 1903 seemed to have left a lasting mark and at no time in the race did he hold out much hope of winning.

The King went racing again on the second day of the meeting and it was noted by a writer of the time that his patronage gave a much-needed boost to the meeting.

Tim Healy, First Govenor of the Irish Free State, congratulating Harry Beasley on riding his own horse Pride of Arras to victory in the Maiden Plate at Punchestown '23. Beasley was then 72.

THE BEASLEY NAME IS SYNONYMOUS WITH PUNCHESTOWN – FROM HARRY THE AGELESS RIDER TO BOBBY A TALENT APART

Raymond Smith

The Beasley name is synonymous with Punchestown. The ageless Harry Beasley, who had six Conyngham Cup successes to his name and was still riding the course at the age of 72 - and winning at that - was unquestionably the doyen of Punchestown horsemen tremendously popular with his legion of admirers. Never did a rider win his way into the affections of the populace as he did.

He was inspired to ride two winners in front of the Prince of Wales when he paid another visit to Ireland and Punchestown in 1885. The Prince had heard of the prowess of this unique character and added personally to the applause as Harry won the Bishopscourt Plate, prompting this description from one writer; "Seldom has the pilot of a successful animal been greeted with such an ovation as met Mr. Harry Beasley on his return to the enclosure."

Harry Beasley... the Prince of Wales was present to see him ride two winners during the afternoon of his visit to Punchestown in 1885.

The Prince of Wales had nothing but total respect for the Beasley name. He asked Harry Beasley to ride Hettie in the 1890 Irish International Handicap Chase at Leopardstown but she failed to get into the frame. Hettie had contested the 1889 Grand National with Magic, also in the Prince's colours but Tommy Beasley won brilliantly on Frigate. It was rather surprising then that the Prince chose Harry as the rider of Hettie rather than Tommy.

Overwhelming Reception

The reception accorded Harry Beasley in 1923 following his success at the age of 72 on the mare Pride of Arras was far more overwhelming. Punchestown overflowed with enthusiasm and emotion. After he had weighed in, the crowd carried him shoulder-high to the Hunt Stand where he was presented to the Governor General, Mr. Tim Healy, and the then Head of the Irish Free State Government, Mr. William T. Cosgrave.

As he replied to the congratulations of Tim Healy, who had been a King's Counsel, remarked: "I'd rather be fighting out a finish with the jockeys over there than be fighting against you in the Law Courts!"

The Governor General, incidentally, had his first ever bet on a horse that day, "investing" in the fortunes of Pride of Arras. So delighted was he to be collecting on the winner that he announced that he would present to the Punchestown meeting a Governor General's Cup (value 200 sovs)

TOMMY BEASLEY... a brilliant rider over the jumps and on the Flat, who had the distinction of beating the immortal Fred Archer in a race. He was 52 when he stepped down from the saddle.

to be competed for by horses owned by regular or reserve officers of any of the recognised armies, navies or air forces of European states.

Harry Beasley's success on Pride of Arras came forty-four years after his initial winning ride at the Festival meeting. (He had the singular record of training and riding Come Away to win the Aintree Grand National in 1891).

In the rain and mud at Punchestown on April 10, 1910, Harry riding St. Columbas, which he trained himself, in the Kildare Hunt Cup came down at the up-bank past the stands.

There was a gasp from the crowd. Beasley remounted and was seen to be last jumping the Big Double. "Beasley is bet", went up the cry from many of those who had backed him as if defeat was out of the question. But he was not "bet". After Vanity Fair had mastered Tyler to look a certain winner at the last, Harry Beasley came with a thrilling run in the last one hundred yards to win by a head.

What a performance by a rider in his 58th year! While he was being cheered all the way to the weighroom, Beasley was heard to remark: "Well, they've not beaten the old fellow yet!".

And still, as they say, he wouldn't lie down. In 1918 he was back again claiming the headlines at Punchestown and as a "veteran of veterans" won the Kildare Hunt Cup on his own horse General Saxham.

In the process he defeated W.J. Parkinson riding More 0'Ferrall's Baltinglass 11 by five lengths. The passage of time was indicated by the fact that one of the younger breed of jockeys, one Joe Canty, already renowned for his prowess on the Flat, showed his versatility by winning the Conyngham Cup on Abou Ben Adam and two other races.

An Audible Silence

In 1924 having ridden Prince of Arras in the Irish Grand National (he was unplaced though completing the course), he was on the same horse in the Prince of Wales's Plate at Punchestown on April 29. The mare fell at the Big Double and gave Beasley what seemed a nasty toss. The audible silence that descended on the crowd showed their deep concern, but happily, the unbreakable Harry was not injured and, as one observer wrote at the time, "it would take more than a tumble to disconcert him".

However, this was the last chase in which he participated. Harry Beasley had ridden for the first time in public on March 21, 1876 - so his career in the saddle lasted 59 years in all.

Against all the odds, Harry Beasley went out with a flourish on the Flat on June 10, 1935 - at the age of 83. In his famous white jacket and blue cap, he rode his four-year-old mare Mollie in the Corinthian Plate at Baldoyle. While he was unplaced, he set a record that will never be surpassed globally - as he passed out the American jockey Levi Barlingame who bade farewell to the racing scene when he rode in his last race at the age of 80 at Stafford, Kansas in 1932.

Five Brothers

The Beasley name is synonymous with the finest traditions of chasing, horsemanship and limitless courage in the saddle.

There were five brothers in all - Tommy, the eldest, then Johnny, Harry, James and Willie. Four would become jockeys but James emigrated and it is not surprising that some articles have conveyed the impression that there were only four instead of five brothers.

All four jockey brothers had the distinction of competing in the Aintree Grand National of 1879, Tommy being placed. Three of them rode in the Grand Nationals of 1880, '84, '87 and '89.

It was at Salisbury House in Athy that Harry Beasley first saw the light of day in 1852.

Growing up within "hailing" distance of some of the most successful stables of the pre-1900 era and also the Curragh and Punchestown tracks, it was not surprising that the Beasleys should catch the riding bug and that in time the history books would record famous victories over the jumps and on the Flat as well.

If Harry was "The Man" because of his level of achievements over four decades, it was his older brother Tommy who had to be rated the most distinguished rider of the quartet.

Just imagine it, having won three Aintree Grand Nationals (1880, '87, and '89), he also won the Irish Derby (1889). And no one managed to break that unique record he created of winning the Aintree Grand National and an Irish Derby in the same year as an amateur and you can bet your last penny that it is a record that is unlikely to be broken in the new Millennium and beyond. Tommy unfortunately didn't have the charisma or the panache of Harry. It was Harry who stirred the imagination of the crowd with his dashing exploits and who stood on a pedestal apart during a lifetime that was unique in the annals of racing.

Harry Beasley's grave in St. Conleth's Cemetery in Newbridge, Co. Kildare.

The Aintree Record

But the careers of the brothers became intertwined when we reflect on the Aintree Grand National. Johnny never managed to get into a place but Tommy, Harry and Willie more than compensated.

The table produced in *Between The Flags* shows that Tommy in addition to his three National wins, was second twice (1878 and '82) and third once (1879), Harry won it in 1891, was a runner-up three times (1883, '85 and '86) and third once (1883) while Willie was second in 1888.

Tommy for his part had only two falls in twelve National rides. Harry fell only once in thirteen rides between 1879 and 1892. In addition to his outstanding record in the National, he won the Grand Sefton Chase four times on Tonans (1880), Lord Chancellor (1881), Zitella (1883) and St. George (1885) and the Grand Hurdle Race at Auteuil on Seaman in 1881.

Standing out like a beacon on the domestic front was that unparalleled record in the Conyngham Cup - six successes in all on Seaman (1881), Frigate (1882), Come Away (1888 and 1889), Lady Helen (1892) and Lively Lad (1905), leaving him three ahead of his brother, Tommy, whose successes were on Christmas Gift (1876), Cork (1886) and Small Talk (1887) while Willie had one victory on Sara Bernhardt in 1891. But what a dominance of one race by one family of riders!

Beat Fred Archer

Tommy's career tended to be overshadowed by the awesome level of Harry's success story and the legend he became in his own lifetime. But Tommy, apart from his achievements as a jump jockey, was a brilliant rider on the Flat and created a special niche for himself by riding against and beating the immortal Fred Archer. And longevity too could be said to be his middle name as he rode in his last race at the age of 52, just seven years shorter than Harry's National Hunt career.

It was at the Leopardstown Second Summer meeting of 1900 that Tommy had his 'Last Hurrah' as a Flat jockey. He had already given up riding as a National Hunt jockey after winning the Kildare Hunt Cup at Punchestown in 1892.

It was fitting in a way that he should step down as a jockey after a memorable battle with his brother Harry. The two of them were competing in the National Hunt Flat Race for the Dublin Plate. Harry, on his own horse, Too Good came out on top by a head and it was recorded in one of the papers of the time that the "set-to between the veteran brothers caused, as may be supposed, the most tremendous excitement among the onlookers".

The Brilliant Henry Linde

Henry Linde, a son of John Hill Linde, will always be linked by those who know the history of the famous Curragh Lodges, with Eyrefield Lodge where he was born in 1835.

Punchestown helped put Linde on the map as a trainer. Early in 1873 he had bought for £25 a seven-year-old mare, Highland Mary who in April of that same year won the Staghunter's Plate at Fairyhouse and eight days later took the Drogheda Stakes at Punchestown. Linde was on the road to the top.

He was ahead of his time in that he laid out a private course at Eyrefield. It was one-and-a-quarter miles long and included every type of fence that a horse had to negotiate on Irish and English courses.

He created a special niche for himself in jumping history when he took two four-year-old horses to Auteuil in France and won the Grand Steeplechase de Paris two years running (1882 and '83). Amazingly, the Auteuil course then included an Irish bank among its obstacles.

His record in the Aintree Grand National would have done justice to Vincent O'Brien who came after him. He took it with Empress in 1880 and again the following year with Woodbrook and he supplied the runner-up three times in Too Good (1886), Martha (1878) and Cyrus (1882). Linde-trained horses won the Sefton Chase at Aintree four times and the record would have been five if Woodbrook in 1879 had not been disqualified on a technicality.

"I'm sorry, my Lord"

But it was at Punchestown that this extraordinary trainer enjoyed his greatest run of success. He won the Conyngham Cup four times and the Prince of Wales's Plate eight times in nine years. In 1883, after his horses had practically swept the board, Linde, according to S.J. Watson in *Between The Flags* was heard to remark when bidding farewell to Lord Drogheda: "I'm sorry, my lord, Punchestown does not continue a few days longer so that I might win some more of your races!".

And adding to his strike rate in the Aintree Grand National, the Sefton Chase, the big jumping races in France and also at the Punchestown meeting, he won the Irish Derby with Pet Fox in 1887 and the Balydoyle Derby five times in all.

If the Beasley brothers were naturals in the saddle, they were fortunate to have come under the wing of brilliant tutors at the vital developing stage of their lives. Tommy was taught by Allen McDonough, Johnny and Willie by J.H. Moore and Harry by the remarkable and legendary Henry Linde himself. The three trainers had their establishments within a stone's throw of one another and their age was a Golden one for Irish racing through the phenomenal strike rate they achieved.

Harry the Trainer

When Harry Beasley himself, on his retirement from the saddle, started training at Eyrefield House in the 1880's it coincided with an extraordinary period of success for Irish horses in the Aintree Grand National. In fact, ten of the eleven winners in the decade from 1889 to 1899 were Irish.

The first top-class chaser to come under his wing was Come-away and Harry Beasley won the Conyngham Cup on him in 1888 and again in 1890. Then in 1891, despite a ligament problem, Come-away gave Harry Beasley victory in the Aintree Grand National, passing the winning post very lame and being retired immediately afterwards. Cloister, ridden by the legendary Captain Roddy Owen was runner-up and Owen gained compensation the following year when he triumphed on Father O'Flynn.

Linde and the Empress

It was a touch of bravura and near recklessness in Henry Lindes make-up that attracted the colourful but tragic Empress Elizabeth of Austria to him. Their relationship was more than merely platonic. She used to come to Ireland incognito for the hunting season and was a frequent visitor to Eyrefield Lodge. Like her sister, the Queen of Naples, she had learned to ride over hurdles without stirrups.

Linde actually named his first Grand National winner, Empress after the Empress of Austria. When he won the Grand Steeplechase de Paris in 1883 the news was immediately telegraphed to Vienna.

Fifteen years on the Empress, who had been undergoing treatment at Nauheim, near Wiesbaden for a heart ailment, was passing through Geneva on her way to Montreux. She put up overnight at a hotel in the city and was on her way to the steamboat on the lake, when she was stabbed by an Italian anarchist with a stiletto that pierced her heart. The story has it that she gallantly walked aboard as if really not badly hurt - but later, she collapsed and died on the spot. One of her riding whips is kept in the headquarters of the Irish Turf Club.

The Second World War was less than two months underway when Harry Beasley passed away at Eyrefield House on October 19, 1939. He was buried in St. Conleth's Cemetery, Newbridge.

His grandson, Bobby Beasley would go into racing history books as one of the greatest and most stylish National Hunt riders in a twenty-year period from 1954-'74 and his success would have been all the greater but for the valley years he endured when battling with the demon drink.

Simply called Bobby

Born Henry Robert Beasley, he was simply called "Bobby" to distinguish him from his father, Henry Herbert Beasley, who in turn was known as Harry or Harry Jnr. to distinguish him from his legendary father, Harry Snr.

Bobby Beasley's father maintained the tradition of jockeyship on the Flat rather than over jumps. Soon after the conclusion of the first World War, he arrived in Britain from Ireland and quickly established himself as a highly-competent rider. For several years he rode for "Atty" Perse's stable and in 1929 won the 2,000 Guineas on Mr. Jinks. His best season was in 1930 when he rode 56 winners.

STYLIST SUPREME... Bobby Beasley winning on P.J. Prendergast's Maddenstown at Punchestown.

Nothing could have been more fitting than that Bobby Beasley should win the Conyngham Cup in 1960 on Fugal Maid, trained by Paddy Sleator.

But, of course, that was overshadowed by his victory on Another Flash in the Champion Hurdle of 1960 for the Sleator stable, his Gold Cup victories on Roddy Owen for Danny Morgan in 1959 and on Captain Christy for Pat Taaffe in 1974 and, most of all, by his Aintree Grand National triumph on the grey Nicolaus Silver for Fred Rimell in 1961, for in this he was emulating his grandfather's victory in 1891.

Amazing Irony

There was an amazing irony in Bobby Beasley winning his first Gold Cup on Roddy Owen. Lord Fingall, a wonderful supporter of National Hunt racing, had named the horse after the distinguished officer and horseman, Captain Roderick (Roddy) Owen.

Harry Beasley as a "vetran of vetrans"

As we have seen already, "New Par" won the Kildare Hunt Cup on his own horse General Saxham.

In the process he defeated W.J. Parkinson riding More O'Ferrall's Baltinglass 11 by five lengths. The passage of time was indicated by the fact that one of the younger breed of jockeys, one Joe Canty, already renowned for his prowess on the Flat, showed his versatility by winning the Conyngham Cup.

A LEGEND IN REPOSE.... Bobbby Beasley says that Captain Christy allowed him to 'retire with dignity'.

"Sleator was a great trainer. He'd school a horse for a year before ever thinking about a race. He was very cute and people would not believe half the stories" said Bobby Beasley.

He described frankly how he had won his battle with alcohol and at 60 was proud to reveal that he hadn't touched a drop for 22 years.

Satanella

The wide-spread fame of the Punchestown races was evident in 1872 when Satanella: A Story of Punchestown was published in Berlin. It was written by G.J. White-Melville, an English novelist and former Coldstream Guards officer, who perhaps had served on the Curragh. The novel told the romantic story of Miss Blanche Douglas, whose nick-name was Satanella, and after whom the mare was named!

When Satanella ran at Punchestown she was described as looking 'as fine as a star. Trained to perfection, her skin shining like satin, her muscles salient, her ribs just visible, her action, though she trotted with rather a straight knee, stealthy, cat-like, as if she were upon wires'.

Alas, as Satanella was in the lead a woman and child fell in front of her causing her to swerve, and to finish in second place.

Retiring with Dignity

"Winning the Gold Cup on Captain Christy was a great moment", he said. "The crowd went mad, some singing *Danny Boy*. I was very open that I had beaten the drink problem. I wanted everybody to know that it could be done. To me there was no stigma to alcoholism".

"Actually, I was too old when I rode Captain Christy and the two defeats he had at Ascot and Haydock would never have happened to me in my heyday. Somehow I sensed that the end was coming but Captain Christy let me retire with dignity. He fell in the Irish Grand National but won the Power Gold Cup four days later. I never rode in public again."

Bobby Beasley made a nostalgic return trip to the Punchestown Festival meeting in '97. He was given red-carpet treatment because the Management realised - as did everyone acquainted with the Festival meeting - the immortality of the links between the Beasley name and Punchestown.

He had rung up Francis Flood to tell him he was coming over. They met for a remembrance of times past in *The Weighroom* in Kilcullen, a haunt of racing men. In the High Noon of his prowess, Bobby Beasley had been unquestionably one of the finest riding talents of all time.

"We talked about the old days and about Paddy Sleator and the planning of victories at Punchestown and other racecourses. There was so much to talk about, so much to recall", said Francis Flood simply.

Two pros who had seen it all, together for an evening of reminiscence.

I would so much have liked to have been with them as the yarns were spun... in the journey back to when Paddy Sleator was "King" of the Punchestown scene.

AT THE KILDARE HUNT BALL.... Mr. and Mrs. William McKeever with Mr. and Mrs. Paddy Sleator in April 1953.

PRINCELY PUNCHESTOWN

This was the opening paragraph of a column and a half account of the Opening Meet of the Kildare Hunt in *The Kildare Observer* on 3rd November 1900: "Whether there is sunshine or showers, the opening meet of the famous 'Killing Kildares' is an event that knows not what neglect is. Kildare people couldn't if they would, and wouldn't if they could, forget the initial gathering of this glorious and historic Hunt. In the centre of the 'sportiest' county in Ireland how could it be otherwise? Imbued to no small extent with sporting proclivities as most of the people in the county are, they are ardently attached to the hunt that has for a century and more enshrined itself in glory, and the fame of which has spread far and near, and about which are associated traditions the cherished thoughts of which, when they rise, swell Kildare's institutions about which and it's offspring, 'Princely Punchestown', the people people cling with a jealous love and care as if it was actually part and parcel of their nature. And perhaps it has become so; if it has it is only what might be expected. Therein lies the secret of its endurance".

6

OTHER GREAT HORSEMEN WHO BECAME IMMORTALISED AT PUNCHESTOWN

The greatest horsemen of each generation from 1850 onwards rode the Punchestown course. Some became immortalised in their own lifetimes because of the amazing level of achievement they attained.

And if we turn the spotlight in particular on the era before the arrival of bush fences, it is only because of the aura created by those specialists who became expert at winning over the awesome bank and stone wall obstacles before the later modifications were introduced.

Names such as Joe Osborne, Francis Flood and P.P. Hogan, to mention but three superb riders who left an indelible imprint in their day, are central to the very lore of Punchestown. Before dwelling on their record-breaking feats, it is fitting that we reflect back on the earliest days and recall some of the timeless characters whose feats still live on in the memory.

A MAGNIFICENT TRIO... Bunny Cox, rated by Martin Molony as "the best amateur rider I saw".

JOE OSBORNE... outstanding horseman who won the Kildare Hunt Cup outright on Alice Whitehorn in 1927.

"The bould Hanway" was how he was dubbed by his peers, who saw him as a hero despite the fact that there were times when the bailiffs seized his horses. And yet he was so much the soul of honour that on one occasion when the horses were taken from him on the eve of a race meeting, he gave an undertaking that they would be returned to the bailiffs immediately the meeting was over - and he was true to his word.

N one more so perhaps than William Hanway who occupied a small farm near the famous Laragh covert. It was said of him that the fact that he died in his bed of a heart attack when close to 70 in 1902 was a miracle in itself as at one time or another he had broken every bone in his body following the hounds and riding in farmer's races all over the country.

He was the last of what one might describe as an exclusive club - that group of sporting farmers of his generation. Before he passed on, he came up with the immortal phrase: "A lot of us used to come out, but drink killed all but me."

P.P. HOGAN... had an amazing Punchestown record and became 'King' of the Hunters Steeplechase.

Severity of Training Methods

At the Punchestown meeting, he could never be left out of the reckoning for the sportsmen's races for Kildare farmers. Indeed, he practically farmed these events as he did the farmers' races at the Fairyhouse meeting and other meetings up and down the country.

Outstanding chasers passed through his hands. But he killed three or four outstanding animals he had in one year in the Eighties because of the unique severity of the training methods he employed. He disdained long ropes and small fences when schooling; rather did he put them over every kind of fence from the outset and even employed a whole parish of men and boys with sticks behind him to ensure that they did not refuse a fence. Those that survived this exacting regime developed into first-rate fencers.

In 1885, seven years before his death, a horse he named John Kane won the Conyngham Cup in his colours. The winning rider was Mr. M.F. Phelan. But Hanway actually rode in a point-to-point race in the year of his death.

Col. St. Leger Moore, a steward of the Irish National Hunt Steeplechase Committee in 1908.

Most Controversial Finish

William Hanway, incidentally, had the distinction of being part of the most controversial finish in the history of Punchestown. It was the second day of the 1892 meeting and the race concerned was the Farmers Challenge Cup, value 50 guineas (presented by Lord Otho Fitzgerald) to which Lord Clonmel added 25 sovs.

It was confined to horses owned by farmers in the Kildare hunting district and was over 3 miles. There were twelve starters, three of which were owned by William Hanway.

Hanway's Tiny Tim, ridden by his owner was first past the post by twelve lengths with Mr. J. Brennan's The Linnet runner-up, Mr. R.H. Tracy's Woodranger third and P. Traynor's Miss Haynestown fourth.

Tiny Tim was objected to for going the wrong course. The Stewards upheld the objection, disqualified Hanway's horse and awarded the race to The Linnet. But the drama did not end there. The owner of Woodranger objected to The Linnet on the grounds of insufficient description and wrong age and he too was disqualified.

Alice Baythorn jumps the last beside Tulyra in the Prince of Wales Plate at Punchestown.

Third Horse Home The Winner!

So the race was awarded to Woodranger, third horse home. Then William Hanway objected to Woodranger on the grounds that his owner was not a bona fide farmer, but this was over-ruled. Another objection to Woodranger for allegedly going the wrong course was also over-ruled.

William Kennedy, second son of Sir John Kennedy, was not alone Master of the Kildare Hunt in the mid-Eighties but a famous rider to hounds and also an outstanding amateur jockey.

Mr. St. James rode the winner of the Kildare Hunt Cup three years running on Confederate (1873-'75) and Capt. Harford won the Conyngham in successive years (1869 and '70) on Wild Fox and Chasseur and then won it a third time as Colonel Harford in 1874 on Milltown, which was successful again the following year but with Mr St. James in the saddle.

The passage of time means, of course, that the names of other renowned riders of that era have faded but they all played their part in adding to the reputation surrounding the great Spring meeting and left tales to be told and retold about the particular races in which they had triumphed.

After the turn of the century, Laurence T. Byrne of Moretown, Donadea claimed to have ridden over Punchestown more often than any other jockey. His first experience of the course was in 1905 and he rode his first winner in 1908. In the early years of the 20th century he rode in every race at each meeting, except, of course, those confined to military personnel and professional jockeys. His proudest memory was of winning the La Touche Cup for Mr. J.C. Kelly, The Mount, Kilcock.

Joe Osbourne, who bred the horse himself, was also the successful rider on that historic day as Alice Whitethorn carrying 13st 3lbs completed the hat-trick and thus won the Kildare Hunt Cup outright. Mrs Osborne is pictured proudly leading in the winner.

Joe Osborne's Lasting Place

The man who became a dominant figure in the Twenties and who was rightly credited with perhaps a better knowledge than anyone else of the peculiarities and vagaries of the Punchestown course was the great J.W. (Joe) Osborne.

One of the fifteen children of a Ballyknockan, Blessington, Co. Wicklow merchant, he always like to recall the day when as a 14-year-old boy, he rode his pony to Punchestown and gazing down from the hills, got his first view of that natural amphitheatre. It stirred something inside him that was never to die. In a word, he was hooked and knew he would never be satisfied until he entered the winner's enclosure.

His courage was a byword. His horsemanship too won him a legion of admirers among the general body of keen judges of National Hunt racing.

One feat alone ensured him a lasting place in the annals of Punchestown - the fact that he rode the winner of the Kildare Cup three years running - 1925, '26 and '27, thus becoming the owner of the trophy outright.

The third success in 1927 was unquestionably the most astounding of all as on his home-bred mare, Alice Whitethorn he defied the welter weight of 13st 3lb over the four mile course.

Of course, Joe Osborne didn't wait until retirement to establish himself as a trainer. In fact, he combined both riding and training with an outstanding strike rate.

Granted a licence in 1920, he saddled his first winner, Beggar's End at Gowran Park in 1921. His Craddoxtown House stable in time was to become famous for the fine National Hunt horses bred - and the winners that flowed from there.

Faithful Following

Not surprisingly, Punchestown became an integral part of his planning each year and, as would be the case with Paddy Sleator later, he had a faithful following who supported him fearlessly.

The 'Alice' name served the Osbornes proudly from that wonderful triumph by Alice Whitethorn in 1927. She was a daughter of the 1914 Galway Plate winner Alice Rockthorn, who produced among others, Alice Maythorn, winner of the Irish Grand National in 1936 and Alice Baythorn who in 1944 took the Punchestown Maiden Plate and the following year won the Prince of Wales Chase over two miles and the Conyngham Cup over four miles. That in itself, revealed a horse of exceptional talent and versatility - to win two such prestigious Punchestown prizes over sharply different distances.

Joe Osborne rode Nell's Son to victory in the Conyngham Cup in 1931 carrying the colours of Mr. Chatier and trained by W.P. Hanly.

It was Aubrey Brabazon who had the mount on Alice Baythorn for Joe Osborne when he won the same race in 1945, carrying the trainer's colours while Martin Molony was his choice of jockey when he turned out National Lad - the grey so popular with Naas race crowds - to win the race again the following year.

Incidentally, in the years of Alice Baythorn's biggest victories he had to compete against the most formidable of opposition, including Lovely Cottage, winner of the Aintree Grand National in 1946 and Lough Con, second to the 100/1 shot Caughoo in the same race in 1947.

Lovely Cottage won the Conyngham Cup in 1944

Initially, when the changes in Punchestown were proposed, Joe Osborne was among those who did not favour them. That in a way was to be expected from one who had come to regard the big banks and the stone wall obstacles as THE real test of horse and rider.

But in time, he came to realise that the change to bush fences was essential, as were the other changes which followed - and he had the vision to be able to applaud them.

Proud Memento

He had one proud memento at the entrance hall to his home that inevitably reminded him and his wife, Helen, of the golden era and, in particular of Alice Whitethorn. It was the solid silver Kildare Hunt Cup standing about three feet high and which writer Sam Weller described in a feature on Punchestown as "one of the most striking sporting trophies I have ever seen".

Tradition Carried On

The Joe Osborne tradition was carried on by his son Paddy, who was brought up steeped in the lore of Punchestown and took over the licence in time from his father.

Paddy confessed to Tom MacGinty, Racing Editor of the *Irish Racing Annual* that "the happiest days of my youth were during the years of the Second World War."

During "The Emergency" years, Craddoxtown House was a three-storey 24-roomed residence and its spacious accommodation was put to full use during the Punchestown meeting each Spring.

"Very few people had their own transport and since we were only a mile down the road from the track, many came to stay from the beginning of the week. The house would be full and there was great excitement for days beforehand."

Later the original house was demolished and gave way to the attractive bungalow that forms the main residence at Craddoxtown House today for Paddy and his wife Joan.

Arrived By Bike

Paddy Osborne clearly recalls P.P. (Pat) Hogan arriving at Craddoxtown the day before the 1942 meeting on his bicycle. Hogan had travelled from Limerick by train, apparently to Sallins, and cycled over to Craddoxtown with his riding gear strapped to his bike.

Already identified as a cross-country rider of unusual talent, P.P. won the Kildare Hunt Cup for Joe Osborne on Silver Cat and had three other winners, including Paddy Sleator's Toy Marine in the Downshire Plate and Tom Dreaper's Slacker in the La Touche Cup.

Paddy Osborne actually started training on the Curragh and moved back to Craddoxtown when his father retired. He made headlines with his father's home-bred Brown Lad in the Sun Alliance Novices Hurdle at Cheltenham in 1974. The horse was sold to the Dreaper stable and was to win three Irish Grand Nationals 1975-'76 and 1978.

Paddy and Joan Osborne in relaxed mood outside their home at Craddockstown, Co. Kildare.

The Third Generation

The family tradition is unlikely to die. Robby Osborne has now taken over his father's licence - so we are now into the third generation. And Robby can be expected to be stirred as his grandfather was when he rode his bicycle to Punchestown that first time and was imbued with the ambition to conquer it first as a rider and later as a trainer. Dan Moore is remembered generally nowadays by the racing fraternity as the man who trained L'escargot to win two successive Cheltenham Gold Cups (1970-'71) and the Aintree Grand National in 1975. His career "bag" of Cheltenham winners was fifteen, putting him third with Edward O'Grady behind Tom Dreaper and Vincent O'Brien. He won the Irish Grand National in 1979 with Tied Cottage.

But he was also an outstanding horseman, whose name will always be linked with Punchestown. And with the era when there was a special type of horse who excelled over its obstacles and at the same time riders with the necessary knowledge and courage to conquer them.

The first meeting after the Second World War was considered one of the greatest in the history of Punchestown. The Spring Festival had held its own despite the restrictions of 'The Emergency' years but 1946 opened a new chapter at the famous Kildare event.

Not alone did Irish racegoers flock to the course that year from every corner of the country intent on enjoying themselves but there was a notable influx of cross-Channel visitors (remember, there were still food shortages in Britain and the promise of a juicy Irish steak after racing was quite a luxury).

Dan Moore Excels

The betting was frenetic in the ring. And the battle for the more prestigious events on the card intense between the leading trainers and riders of the time. Dan Moore excelled in recording a double on the first day with Revelry and Drogheda and was runner-up on Jackie Brown in the Prince of Wales Plate beaten by Jack O'Down (Capt. Baggally) who was the medium of a tremendous gamble. The 'Punchestown Roar' that greeted this success showed that the confidence in the gelding was fully justified.

Dan Moore got an equally rousing reception as he came back in after winning the Maiden Plate from a big field on Revelry and in the last race he steered Drogheda to victory over the Paddy Sleator-trained Ballylan. While Moore's horse was well backed, there was significant support for Father Time, the mount of Jimmy Brogan.

Dan Moore was on the favourite, Savina in the Tickell Cup but victory went to stable companion Pekeisko, who led from start to finish.

The second day saw him triumph easily in the Kildare Hunt Plate on the favourite Silent Prayer from the Paddy Sleator stable. Random Knight (Ernie Newman), trained by Tom Dreaper for Lord Bicester was runner-up.

Arthur Maintains Highest Standards

Arthur Moore certainly maintained at the very highest level the standards set by his father, and nowhere was this more evident than at Cheltenham where he had the distinction of winning the Arkle Challenge Trophy with Klairon Davis in 1995 while the same horse won the Queen Mother Chase the following year.

Klairon Davis in his prime was an outstanding Spring horse and a great favourite with the Punchestown crowds. He won the £50,000 BMW Handicap Chase (two miles) with Fran Woods in the saddle in successive years (1996 and 1997). In 1997 carrying 12 st he had eight lengths to spare over Nicky Henderson's Big Matt.

The Brabazon Ties

The Brabazon family ties with Punchestown go back a long time - back to the era when Cecil Brabazon, father of Aubrey was one of the doyens of the Irish racing scene, especially as a trainer of note. Cecil too, started his racing career as a jockey and had his first ride at Punchestown in 1910. Indeed, his record there was a remarkable one and he won the Downshire five times in all.

His first victory was on Nella's Favour, trained by the late Michael Dawson, father of Michael Dawson; he then won it two years running on horses trained by the late James Ballesty - Glascorn and Jamestown. He won the Conyngham Cup of 1912 on Repeater 11.

As a trainer Cecil had an equally impressive string of successes at Punchestown and trained a couple of Conyngham Cup winners including Ballyhooley which won in '40.

Of course, Aubrey Brabazon will invariably be linked in the minds of old-timers with one horse when they reflect on his association with the Festival meeting - and that is Alice Baythorn, the famous mare, referred to already, that was trained by Joe Osborne. Aubrey rated 'Alice' as one of the best jumpers he ever sat on and little wonder. She carried him to victory on the first day of the 1945 meeting in the Prince of Wales's Plate and there was general acclaim for the beautiful ride "The Brab" gave her (Lough Conn, though well fancied, was not concerned with the finish).

Most Popular Ever

The next day, carrying a 7lbs penalty, she scored a smooth and clear-cut victory from ten others in the four-mile Conyngham Cup. Lovely Cottage had a big following but was unplaced as the cheers of the crowd for Aubrey Brabazon and the brave mare rocked the stands and enclosures. Indeed, there were unforgettable scenes as 'Alice' returned to the winner's enclosure. It was a real Punchestown ovation, marking one of the most popular wins ever at the meeting. Aubrey Brabazon, of course, shared in the enthusiastic congratulations and deservedly so, as on each day, his handling of the mare was flawless.

"The Brab" rode Cottage Rake to three successive Cheltenham Gold Cups 1948-'50 for Vincent O'Brien and was associated with the 1950 and '51 Champion Hurdle victories of Hatton's Grace, Tim Molony having the mount when the three-timer was recorded in 1952.

It was as a Flat jockey with a wonderful pair of hands and superb judgement in a finish that many will remember Aubrey Brabazon. There is a famous photo of Prince Aly Khan leading in the Aga Khan's Masaka, with Aubrey up, after she had won the Irish Oaks of 1948.

There is no smile on the Prince's face and the reason behind that dark look was that he had a substantial bet on his own filly, Amino ridden by Morny Wing. Amino had to be satisfied with second place.

Martin Molony's name does not figure as prominently among the riders who were consistent annual winners at Punchestown as one might expect, though he did - as we have seen already - ride National Lad to victory for Joe Osborne in the 1946 Conyngham Cup (he actually had a retainer with Joe). The reason for this is that Martin's talents both as a National Hunt and Flat jockey were so much in demand in Britain. Indeed, he confessed to me in the course of an interview I did with him for the 1987-'88 *Irish Racing Annual* that his body "could not stick the pace of the non-stop whirlwind life" that started for him in 1948 and went on until that fateful day at Thurles on September 18th in 1951 when a cruel fall on Bursary in the Munster Chase (which saw him suffer a fractured skull) ended his career prematurely at 26.

Could Not Stick Pressure

"My body could not stick it, the pressure on the nervous system was intense", he added. There was his *mano a mano* with Joe Canty - "the best rider in Ireland in my day" - in three of the five Irish Classics in 1946, followed by his duel first with the legendary Morny Wing and then with 'The Flying Scotsman' Tommy Burns in 1947. In the Irish 1,000 Guineas that season, Martin Molony on Desert Drive went under by a short head to Morny Wing on Sea Symphony after a tremendous battle. In the Irish Oaks Martin again had the mount on Desert Drive and this time beat Tommy Burns on Isabelline by three-quarters-of-a-length.

THE INCOMPARABLE MARTIN MOLONY... third from left, won the Conyngham Cup twice at Punchestown, on National Lad in 1946 for Joe Osborne and on Hasty Bits in 1950 for Tom Dreaper. He is pictured here holding the Cheltenham Gold Cup at a dinner in Fitzpatrick's Hotel Killiney in 1998 to celebrate the 75th anniversary of the Cup which he won on Silver Frame in 1951. Also pictured from left: Tommy Carberry (L'Escargot 1970/ '71), Dessie Hughes (Davy Lad '77), Willie Robinson (Mill House '63) and Frank Berry (Glencaraig Lady '72).

It was not enough for Martin Molony to pit his genius and his skill against Joe Canty, Morny Wing and Tommy Burns in the Irish classics and other big races. In the 1950 English Oaks the line-up of jockey talent as they passed the finishing line was - 1st Asmena (W.R. Johnstone), 2nd Plume 11 (E.C. Elliott), 3rd Stella Polaris (M. Molony) and La Baille (C. Smirke).

One of the Best-Ever Chase Jockeys

Bob Curling, most respected of English racing writers in his day, said of Martin Molony: "I must rate Martin Molony as one of the very best-ever steeplechase jockeys. I am not sure that everyone realises just how brilliant a rider he was."

John Welcome, writing in his book *The Cheltenham Gold Cup* in relation to Martin Molony's Gold Cup win on Silver Fame said: "Molony's brilliance from the last fence home was never seen to better advantage, and the old horse may well have owed the crowning achievement of his career as much to his jockey's strength and genius as to his own courage and refusal to admit defeat."

Changing At Crewe

Martin Molony would leave Dublin by boat at the start of the week and find himself, sometimes on a bleak winter's morning during the National Hunt season, changing at Crewe to get to the particular track where he had the first of his cross-Channel rides of the week. The one concession he made to a regime that must have been so exacting to his frame was that he would fly home on Friday evenings to be sure that he would be back in time to ride in Ireland on the Saturdays.

He rode in America during holiday breaks - and rode very successfully - and in France too. And flights were much slower and much less comfortable then than they are now.

"I never asked for a ride in my life", he said. At the peak of his powers, he didn't have to. Men sought him out. He was in constant demand, day in, day out."

Apart from the Conyngham Cup victory on National Lad for Joe Osborne in 1946, he won the same race for Tom Dreaper on Hasty Bits.

Molony greatly admired a Limerick neighbour and veterinary surgeon Capt. John O'Grady. "He was a beautiful horseman and rode to work every morning until of an advanced age". The Captain's dedication had its rewards over a long period at Punchestown, where he twice won the Governor General's Cup outright. Brown Ivy first did the trick for him from 1925 to 1927. She completed a four-timer in the event in 1928 and fell the following year, but O'Grady made the new trophy his own when Old Tim scored for him in 1932 and '33, and thereafter there was no Governor General.

The Best Amateur

Much as O'Grady was admired, Martin Molony believes J.R. (Bunny) Cox was the best amateur rider he saw. There are few who would dispute the opinion. First coming to prominence on the horses trained by his father at Lisnawilly outside Dundalk, Bunny quickly made his mark. He was in demand from all the leading stables and at the height of his career was riding about 20 point-to-point winners a season for Paddy Sleator, and could hold his own with the professionals at the highest level. He won both the Two Miles Champion Chase and Cathcart Cup on Quite Que for Dan Moore at Cheltenham.

Four Winners In The Same Afternoon

In 1949 he rode four winners on the same afternoon at Punchestown, including the Conyngham Cup on Loyal Antrim, a feat that was not equalled until Tommy Carmody booted home four winners, three of them trained by John Mulhern on the final afternoon of the 1990 Festival. With typical modesty, Bunny Cox responded to a reminder of that notable day 50 years ago: "Shortly before that I rode four favourites at Punchestown and they all fell", and he then proceeded to direct attention away from the rider to the horses. Most particularly to Little Trix, the diminutive grey with the heart of a lion.

A prolific winner over hurdles, she appeared to love jumping banks and in 1951 won the Prince of Wales Chase and the Conyngham Cup.

Five years later Highland Trout, ridden by Bunny, won the Punchestown Cup and the La Touche. This was the same breed as Little Trix, who went on to breed eight foals. All were good winners with perhaps the best, Four Trix, a stout stayer, winning the Scottish National.

Ted Walsh on the P.P. Hogan-trained Any Crack side-steps the faller, Killinick King (David O'Connor) at the Double Bank and goes on to victory in the La Touche Cup at Punchestown '84.

P.P. Hogan's Amazing Record

P.P. Hogan did not ride all that many winners during a restricted career, he was confined by the Stewards from an early stage to amateur races. Nonetheless he was champion amateur in 1946, had a career total of 35 winners from only 95 rides under Rules, and on one occasion rode eleven consecutive point-to-point winners.

King of the Hunter's Chase

In later years as an owner and trainer Pat Hogan became King of the Hunters' Steeplechases dominating the class at Punchestown from 1979 until the Nineties, with horses such as Any Crack, Under Way, Ah Whist and Howyanow. Any Crack won both the Ladies Cup and La Touche in 1979 and the La Touche at four subsequent fixtures, ridden initially by Niall Madden and then Ted Walsh. Under Way won the Champion Hunters Chase in '79, '80 and '84. Caroline Beasley's brilliant Eliogarty relegated him into second place in 1985, depriving Hogan of training seven consecutive winners of this prestige event. He saddled Ah Whist to win it four times between '86 and '90 with Howyanow filling in in 1988.

Howyanow had emulated Any Crack by winning the Ladies Plate and La Touche in 1987 and also landed the La Touche in '89 and '90. The mounts at that stage on Hogan's horses falling variously to Enda Bolger, the trainer's son-in-law, and Roger Hurley.

Cycled To Punchestown

Pat Hogan was not the only rider during the war years to fall back on the old reliable bicycle. In 1944, Martin Molony was faced with the problem of getting to Punchestown only a few weeks after he had won the Irish Grand National on Knight's Crest when still a teenager. "In those days, I stayed all the time with Capt. Cyril Harty at Chapelizod" recalled Martin.

"My brother Tim came up by train from Limerick, spent the night with us and on the Tuesday he and I cycled to Punchestown on a bicycle made for two."

Enterprise Poorly Rewarded

Martin's enterprise was poorly rewarded for he got a nasty fall from a horse called Pucka Man in the Prince of Wales Chase. "Amazingly that was the only occasion during my career that I broke a collarbone - poor Jimmy Brogan I think had about 19 fractures. However, it was some consolation that I got a ride back in the ambulance to St. Vincent's Hospital, where they kept me for a couple of days. Poor Tim had to pedal the tandem back to Chapelizod on his own".

Martin was fortunate that there was an actual ambulance available to bring him to hospital. Nowadays no race meeting can start unless there are at least two ambulances, or recovery vehicles, available. Often that was not feasible in the Forties, a fact of which the late Jack Doyle was made all too painfully aware.

P.P. Hogan receives the Manor Inn Ladies Cup from Mr and Mrs Dennis Curry after his Howyanow had won in the hands of Mr R. Hurley at Punchestown '87. The same horse won the La Touche Cup and was triumphant in the Champion Hunters event in 1998 and again in 1999.

Jack's Experience

He was not too sure of the name of the horse as he related the story to me, but the records suggest that it was Vestige which he partnered in the La Touche on the same day that Molony got his tumble. In any event, Jack remembered tracking two leaders to the Double Bank. "A few strides off, the pair came together. My horse had no view of the bank, crashed into the top and I landed on the other side, on my back, on the lip of the ditch". Fortunately Doyle, who went on to become an eminently successful bloodstock agent, was a very fit man, being in addition to his equine activities, a champion sprinter and an international rugby player. Otherwise he might not have survived a prolonged and uncomfortable journey to hospital.

THE DIMINUTIVE GREY WITH THE HEART OF A LION...
Bunny Cox comes in on Little Trix after winning
the Conyngham Cup in 1951.

Peter Scudamore's brilliant British champion jump jockey in his prime and to-day a well-known television personality, experiences a moment of frustration at Punchestown '87 as Hazy Sunset falls at the last with victory within sight.

"They had to carry me back to the weighroom (a long way from the double bank) on the wing of a hurdle. I lay in the weighroom until nearly eight o'clock that evening when Willie Beasley managed to get hold of a fellow with a van. At that point I had no feeling in my legs, and they slid me into the van and drove me to Surgeon Barniville in Dublin. He got me into hospital and fortunately the injury proved to be less serious than it first appeared.

The Beasleys and the Floods, the Dreapers, T.W. and his son Jim, the Taaffe's, Rathcoole trainer Tom, his celebrated sons, Toss, Willie and the late Pat and his grandson Tom; Capt. Cyril Harty and his sons Buster, Eddie and the much-missed John, Paddy Mullins and his offspring, notably Willie and Tony and the Osbornes, which brings us back to where we started.

The Punchestown achievements of Francis Flood and Bobby Coonan are covered in the following chapter because they are irretrievably linked with the golden Paddy Sleator era.

It is amazing how the Punchestown tradition has been carried on down through certain noted families. And so it will go on into the new Millennium. Ruby Walsh, Irish champion jump jockey in 1999 at the age of 20 has taken up the reins of his father Ted and had a major success over the course in 1999 when winning the Heineken Gold Cup Chase on Imperial Call. And Paul Carberry carries on the legacy of his grandfather Dan Moore while Fran Flood ensures that people will not forget all the success achieved by his father, Francis. The cycle is a perennial one.

7

WHEN PADDY SLEATOR WAS 'KING': A TOTAL OF 32 FESTIVAL WINNERS OVER A FOURTEEN YEAR SPAN

To-day in Grangecon in the Garden County of Wicklow you can still see the house from which Paddy Sleator, like a born Commander-in-Chief, planned with consummate detail his annual assault on the Punchestown Festival meeting. He had the enviable strike rate of turning out 32 winners over a fourteen-year span from 1950 to '63. There was not one blank year in all that time.

There were Festival meetings that were truly special. Special, like the pinnacle year of 1958 when he produced his second five-timer, Francis Flood riding four of them.

I paid a nostalgic visit to the village in March, 2000 just to get a 'feel' of what it must have been like when everything revolved around the Sleator success story, just as it did in Churchtown, Co. Cork when Vincent O'Brien made it his base for his initial onslaught on Cheltenham, where his record was unmatched over a ten-year span.

STARTED OUT AS AN OUTSTANDING AMATEUR RIDER... The youthful trainer Paddy Sleator with Skenhanagh after he had won the Downshire Plate at Punchestown 1994.

Paddy Sleator in the pose by which many people will remember him, smoking his inevitable cigarette through that long holder of his.

LIKE FATHER LIKE SON... Francis Flood, who was to become a successful trainer after an outstanding career in the saddle had happy rapport with Paddy Sleator, and has reason to be proud to-day of the achievements of his son Fran as a rider.

For months beforehand Punchestown would be the one topic of conversation on everyone's lips. Everything seemed to stop during the meeting itself. Hard to believe it now, but even though Punchestown was only fifteen miles away, few people had cars as is the case to-day. It meant that for the majority, the train was the popular means of transport.

Francis Flood recalled in an interview with Tom MacGinty in the *Irish Racing Annual* the immense interest that was generated in one small community. "It seemed as if the entire village was crammed on to the platform, below at the station, waiting for the train to Naas and from there they would take a bus or a char-a-banc over to Punchestown. Even after the railway was discontinued, buses or coaches were organised from the village. The two days were great outings".

I find myself gravitating to Moore's pub, the proverbial stone's throw from the Sleator homestead, and which naturally became the centre of great celebrations as the Sleator-trained horses hit the headlines and the locals came home to enjoy their winnings. Old timers who lived through those times remember them as 'golden days' that could never be repeated. When the intensity of the celebrations - with talk of horses and individual races, of outstanding feats and horsemanship, the repartee, the craic and the singing - had abated, there would be card sessions extending through the night and into the dawn. No one apparently wanted the fun to stop.

Noel Moore, popular and well-known proprietor of Moore's pub, had passed on during the previous twelve months and now the establishment is run by his widow Mary and very likeable son, Paul, who gave me some old newspaper cuttings that conjured up highlights of the Sleator years. I could not but notice at the same time, the old print taking up most of one wall of a cricket team in full regalia - the Grangecon side of 1924! Such an anomaly could only occur in an Irish pub but then the British had brought cricket with them and many a hamlet had its own team. To this day, sports editors in Irish daily, evening and Sunday papers will confess to you that when England are playing Australia for the Ashes, they would leave out the latest score at their peril.

But it was racing, not cricket that made Grangecon famous far beyond the shores of Ireland. And wherever lovers of the National Hunt game gather to talk about great horses and great trainers the name of Paddy Sleator and Grangecon invariably spring to mind.

Sleator was brought up with an ingrained love of horses. Fate stepped in to put him first on the road to be a jockey and then a trainer. He suffered a bout of rheumatic fever when he was nine and, after recovering, the doctor advised that he should ride a pony each day round the fields and hills of the family farm. He graduated to gymkhanas and a little later to hunting and point-to-point riding at which he excelled. In 1927 he received his amateur rider's licence.

He was to prove himself an outstanding amateur who in 1934 and 1938 topped the list of riders in that sphere, while in 1937 he shared the title with Tim Hyde,

who subsequently turned professional, winning the 1939 Aintree Grand National on Workman and in addition became the brilliant Prince Regent's regular partner.

Paddy Sleator was only 20 years old when he took out a trainer's licence and scored his first Punchestown success with Silver Linnet, ridden by himself in the Ladies Cup in 1933. In addition to Silver Linnet, the only other winner he rode at Punchestown was That's Him in the Punchestown Cup in 1935. It may appear a surprising statistic but he was such a polished horseman - riding up there in the Bunny Cox league - that the Stewards saw fit to restrict him and other amateurs from riding in any but amateur races.

Sleator's experience in the saddle made him very selective in his choice of jockeys. The list of those who rode winners for him at Punchestown speaks for itself. Tim Hyde was one of them. Others include P.P. Hogan, Bunny Cox, Dan Moore, Pat Taaffe, Francis Flood, the trainer's cousin C. Noel Sleator and Timmy Jones.

And, of course, he utilised to the full the unique talent of Bobby Beasley when he was in his prime. It was Beasley who rode Another Flash to victory for him in the Champion Hurdle of 1960.

DAYS WHEN SLEATOR DOMINATED THE RACING HEADLINES... The old newspaper cuttings show the days of dominance enjoyed by Paddy Sleator in his prime with Francis Flood and himself chosen as Sports Stars of the Week after they shared in five winners from five runners.

When the association with Bobby Beasley ended, along came Bobby Coonan. He struck up a partnership with the Master Of Grangecon that produced an awesome stream of winners, including some of the most prestigious prizes in the Irish racing calendar

Bobby Coonan was born in 1939 at Ballymore Eustace near Grangecon and he established a lasting rapport with Sleator who, as we have seen, was a true-blue perfectionist. Coonan shared his first Irish jockey's championship while with Sleator and then from 1967-1972 took six championships in succession.

During the collection of those championships he rode the winner of virtually every big chase in Ireland. And for him the Galway Plate was a particularly happy race as he won it three times; twice on Royal Day and once on O'Leary. But the Aintree Grand National was the illusive one.

"I had seven rides in it and never got around, most of the time I was knocked over by loose ones or fallers, and got so frustrated with the place that I could have become an instant vandal and burned Liverpool to the ground".

Other English tracks were more kind and he included the King George Chase on Captain Christy among his takings there as well as sharing in the Cheltenham win of Ballywilliam Boy. But it was in Ireland that he made his real mark, and this was as he wanted it.

Francis Flood was moulded by Sleator to reach the very top of the ladder in his prime.

There were, as Tom MacGinty pointed out in the *Irish Racing Annual* feature on Paddy Sleator, close ties between the two families. With farms on either sides of Grangecon, Francis Flood's father, who bred and raced a few horses from his Rock Farm, gave Sleator his initial experience, and while Sleator later moved up country to ride for a relative, John Wilson of Kilternan, before

setting up on his own, it seemed natural that, following the death of Tom Flood, the youthful Francis would be taken on by Paddy Sleator. More particularly because the natural banks that were a feature of the Flood farm, comprised a splendid schooling ground for Punchestown, and one regularly availed of by Sleator.

Flood never looked back from 1953. He rode at least one winner at every Festival up to and including 1962. In 1957 he rode two for his brother Tom, training on the family farm, and two for Sleator who produced his second five-timer the following year. Francis Floood was on four of them and rode a fifth on Clarestown, trained by Padge Berry, in the Courtown Plate.

Francis Flood finds it difficult to nominate the best of the many good horses he rode around Punchestown, but he has no doubt which was the fastest, Sleator's Monk's Star in the 1957 four miles Maiden Plate. "There were only four runners and he took off from the start. He was a head-strong individual and no horse ever covered the first two miles at Punchestown faster than he did. He flew the banks. Breathtaking. He was later sold to England and I believe was killed there. English type racing would not have suited him".

The Pinnacle

The year 1958 was the pinnacle of the Sleator-Flood partnership at Punchestown, but the following year provided Flood with a reminder of what a cruel mistress racing can be, and the rest of us with further evidence of what a tough breed National Hunt riders are. Following a crashing fall at Fairyhouse, Francis ended up in the Mater Hospital. Fears that he had suffered a serious back injury happily proved groundless, but there was no doubt Francis had a broken wrist, the x-ray revealing a distinct gap between the two parts of severed bone.

Flood was out for an indefinite period, and Punchestown looked a non starter. The heavy plaster was removed a few days before the meeting, but he was still bound and grounded when he went as a spectator, he thought, for day one. But brother Tom, seeing him on the spot, assumed Francis was going to ride his Nice Gift in the Bishopscourt Cup and was so enthusiastic that Francis had not the heart, nor the desire, to disillusion him.

Despite being virtually one armed, Flood performed well and Nice Gift romped home to set up a hat-trick for the Flood brothers. Nice Gift scored again in 1960 and for good measure Francis rode Nice Gift to victory in the Conyngham Cup of 1962.

The Downturn

The subsequent downturn in Sleator and Flood's strike rate at Punchestown had nothing to do with the rider's injury, nor the introduction of the bush fence course in 1960, which directly limited the opportunities for the banks specialists. It was more a reflection of Paddy Sleator's disenchantment with the Irish racing authorities' failure to provide opportunities for young horses, and to restrict bumper winners access to Flat Handicaps, in which Sleator had made a number of killings.

The trainer decided to transfer his best horses to Arthur Thomas' yard in Warwickshire, along with their lads and stable jockey Bobby Beasley who otherwise would have ridden more than three Punchestown winners for the stable. Sleator himself masterminded their training and programmes, and the strike rate over a five year period was phenomenal.

Remarkable Results

Paddy Sleator, who had been Champion Trainer in Ireland in 1958, and in each of the seven years from 1955 to 1961 trained more winners than any other trainer, undertook another major overseas operation in 1968, sending seven horses to Cagnes-Sur-Mer to beat the restrictions on racing imposed because of a foot-and-mouth epidemic in Ireland. Once more he achieved remarkable results.

Ballywilliam Boy in 1971 was Sleator's last Cheltenham winner. In 1976 O'Leary, also ridden by many times Champion stable jockey, Bobby Coonan, won Sleator his ninth Galway Plate. The following year Four Kings and Mr. Timmy Jones became the trainer's sixth winner of the Bishopscourt Cup and Paddy Sleator decided to call it day.

Flood Makes His Mark

By then, Francis Flood had held a trainer's licence for ten years and he and his wife Teresa were well established in their new home, Ballynure on the sylvan slopes outside Grangecon. It was no surprise when Francis struck early with Rita's Pet in the Ladies Cup of 1967, but the newcomer hit the headlines in a big way in 1970.

RECALLING THOSE GOLDEN TIMES... Francis Flood, right and Bobby Coonan (centre) shares reminisances of the Sleator era with the late Noel Moore, proprietor of Moore's Pub in Grangecon. This picture was taken in March 89.

Flood's young stars progressed to Punchestown where Garoupe won the Guinness Handicap Chase and Glencaraig Lady the top novice event, the John Jameson Gold Cup, both ridden by Ben Hannon.

The following season Glencaraig Lady was again out of luck at Cheltenham falling in the Gold Cup, but twelve months later, with Flood's new stable jockey Frank Berry, freshly recruited from the ranks of leading Flat race apprentices, in the saddle, Glencaraig Lady won gold at Cheltenham.

Meanwhile, Francis Flood continued to maintain his enviable strike rate at Punchestown, adding two more Guinness Handicaps, a Downshire Hurdle, the BMW Champion Novice Hurdle and with another brace of Bishopscourt Cups added to the tally, there is no surer mark of the passage of time than to find the next generation in the form of Mr. F.J. (Fran) Flood among the Punchestown honours. Indeed Fran has shown , as would be expected, from his very breeding, natural talent in abundance and a penchant for producing the goods on the big occasion.

Today Paddy Sleator's former home and yard is no longer a racing establishment but has been incorporated by his daughter Diane and her husband David Nagle into their outstandingly successful Barronstown Stud.

Paddy had a great sartorial sense, cutting a distinctive dash in his carefully-tailored suits topped with tribly, smoking the inevitable cigarette through that long holder of his.

He was feared by the bookies as a master of the shrewd "touch". His faithful band of followers had complete faith in him when the money was down. But, amazingly, while there was no better man to place a horse to win and see to it that it delivered when "on the job", he didn't bet heavily himself, as many would have thought. Coming up to a race, though he knew everything he should have done in preparation had been done, he would suddenly find a hundred reasons why the horse in question could fail. He was too cautious by far ever to get involved in serious confrontation with the layers, though naturally he would have an "interest" flutter.

It was his friends who "went to war" in the ring and set the scene alight when he gave the word that one was ready.

When he celebrated his 80th birthday in February, 1989, quite a number of his close pals gathered to celebrate with him including Jack Doyle, P.P.Hogan, Jack (Boiler) White, Ted Curtin, Michael Purcell and Michael Fitzgibbon of Thurles. You can imagine what an evening of racing yarns that produced.

I only wish I could have been there with a tape-recorder...

The legacy of Paddy Sleator and Punchestown will never die and Grangecon will always be the little village where his spirit hovers for racing men.

A Punchestown Landmark

One of the most historic of all Punchestown landmarks is the famous standing stone near the 'Dublin Gap' gate entrance which was re-erected vertically in 1934. A small Bronze Age burial cist was found nearby.

It stands 19½ feet high and is made of granite, a material which is foreign to the district the nearest granite being found at Ballyknockan in County Wicklow.

The finding of the cist close by suggests the idea of a monument to the dead. In ancient Irish Law Tracts such stones are referred to as Stones of Adoration - a possible pointer to their use as images or altars. The religious nature of the stone is further demonstrated by their being found at places where rituals were performed.

The conversion of the monuments to Christian use may represent attempts to incorporate and adapt older non-Christian traditions into the new faith. Other theories for the original existence of the longstones are that they were intended to commemorate events of importance in the locality or simply to serve as landmarks, sites of roadways or boundary marks. Monuments contemporaneous with longstones are the numerous stone forts, dolmens and massive burial chambers. In general, such monuments belong to the period 2,000 - 500 B.C.

THE CONYNGHAM CUP

In 1865, the Marquess of Conyngham, whose grandmother had done so much to entertain King George IV on his visit to Ireland in 1821, presented the Conyngham Cup of 300 sovereigns in *specie* added to a sweepstakes of 5 sovereigns each. The first race was run over the Old Course, about four miles, on 20 April 1865, and was won by Mr. J. Lannigan's 'General Election' ridden by Mr. Gavacan. As the *Irish Times* recorded on 17 April: "Subsequent to the result of the Conyngham Cup race, his Royal Highness the Prince of Wales and Prince Teck, accompanied by Lord Mayo and several gentlemen of the Kildare Hunt, rode round the course, saw the horses starting and then galloped across the plain to see them cross the double fence".

From Col. S.J. Watson, "Between the Flags".
A history of Irish Steeplechasing 1969.

*The Kildare Hunt provided horsemen who revelled in the challenge of Punchestown fences,
and the Kildare Hunt Cup was the race that they were often most anxious of all to win.*

*The old Double bank always fascinated the artist and this historic print captures
those in the field who survived and the ones that came to grief.*

THE START OF THE CONYNGHAM CUP AT PUNCHESTOWN 1872

Left to Right: Mr Whyte (Bashful), Mr G Moore (Curragh Ranger), Mr Comerford (Chisel),
Mr. Exshaw (Quickstep), Captain McCalmont (Magenta), Mr Oldham (Ireland Yet),
Mr St James (Lamp), Mr. Thomas (Star of the Sea), Captain Smith (Heraut D'Armes),
Mr Beasley (Hubert), Mr Long (Ruric), Captain MacFarlane (Waterford).

PAINTED BY J. STURGESS
ENGRAVED BY E.G. HESTER

THE CONYNGHAM CUP AT PUNCHESTOWN 1872

Left to Right: Captain Smith (Heraut D'Armes), Mr Moore (Curragh Ranger), Mr Thomas (Star of the Sea), Mr Whyte (Bashful), Captain MacFarlane (Waterford), Mr Beasley (Hubert), Mr Comerford (Chisel), Mr StJames (Lamp), Mr Oldham (Ireland Yet), Captain McCalmont (Magenta).

PAINTED BY J. STURGESS
ENGRAVED BY E.G. HESTER

THE FINISH OF THE CONYNGHAM CUP AT PUNCHESTOWN 1872

Left to Right: Captain Smith (Heraut D'Armes), Mr G Moore (Curragh Ranger), Mr Whyte (Bashful),
Captain MacFarlane (Waterford), Mr Beasley (Hubert), Mr Thomas (Star of the Sea),
Mr St James (Lamp).

PAINTED BY J. STURGESS
ENGRAVED BY E.G. HESTER

*A painting by Henry Barraud made
from the drawings of Mr. J. O'Hea
and based on the Chancellor photographs
of the meeting of 1868 when
the Prince of Wales attended. He is shown,
centre, in white coat greeting the crowd.
The picture hangs in the Drawing Room
of the Shelbourne Hotel, Dublin.*

THE CHALLENGE AND THE GLORY...

Two magnificent paintings by Gilbert Halliday of Punchestown in 1930, showing the field taking the formidable stone wall fence as it was then and horses negotiating the Double Bank.

We'd better have a look at the form...

There's plenty of time to get down to the rails...

We'd better get a move on. The race starts in ten...

We could always watch it here in the bar...

The last word in beer.

*Providing the Setting for Special Events
and Corporate Entertainment*

Western Pleasure Tuam Ltd

Western Pleasure Tuam Ltd., Tel: 093 24472. Fax: 093 24079. Email: johnfahy@indigo.ie

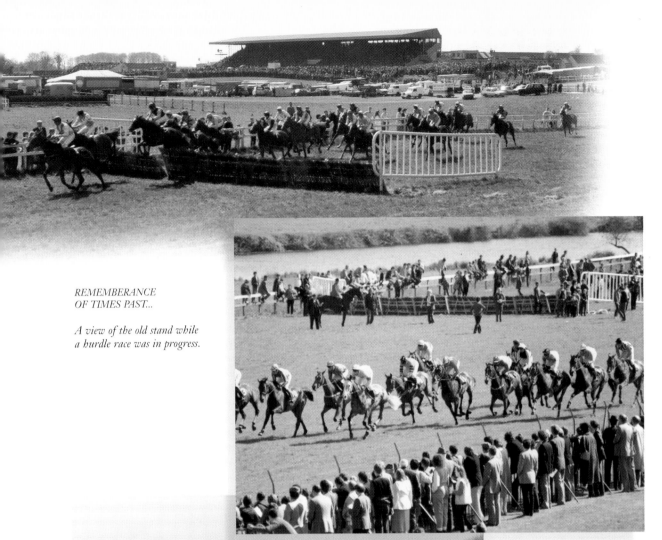

REMEMBERANCE
OF TIMES PAST...

*A view of the old stand while
a hurdle race was in progress.*

The start of a Steeplechace.

*The Parade Ring as it was before the advent of the new
£8.75 million complex in 1998.*

Families arrive waiting their turn
to savour the joy of the swing while four
girls are content to relax on the grass
as the jazz band plays it cool.

The fun fair retains its eternal appeal
but these four men are concerned more
with picking a winner.

Cox's Cash & Carry

Newbridge & Thurles

Supporters of Punchestown for over 50 Years

"A Traditional way of doing Business"
DERMOT COX, *Managing Director*

Friendly, Efficient, Professional & Good Value

For all your wholesale needs contact us at:

Thurles Cash & Carry
Racecourse Road
Thurles, Co. Tipperary
Tel: 0504 22076
Fax: 0504 23549

Cox's Cash & Carry
Newbridge Industrial Estate
Newbridge, Co. Kildare
Tel: 045 431594
Fax: 045 431386

Jumping The Old Double in the Cox's Cash & Carry Steeplechase for the La Touche Cup

FOURTH RACE

4.25 p.m.   2½ m.

THE JOHN JAMESON CUP. A Perpetual Challenge Cup presented by John Jameson and Son, Ltd. A sweepstakes of 5 sovs each with 4 sovs extra if not struck out on 17 April (total liability 9 sovs), with 1,000 sovs added, of which the second 15 per cent. and the third 10 per cent of the whole stakes. The winner will receive 75 per cent. and the Jameson and Son, Ltd. A weight for age steeplechase for four years old and upwards that have not won a steeplechase on or before 1st November 1962. Weights—Four years old 10st 13lb; six years old and aged, 11st 6lb. Penalties—The winner of a steeplechase to carry 4lb extra; five years old, 10st 13lb; of a steeplechase value 400 sovs or steeplechases collectively value 250 sovs, 7lb extra; of a steeplechase value 600 sovs or steeplechases collectively value 800 sovs, 12lb extra. Value to winner £856 15 0; second £172 7 0; third £114 18 6.

ABOUT TWO MILES AND A HALF OVER BUSH FENCE COURSE

Rid:			age	st	lb		Trainer
114	1—FLYING WILD	Gr m by Airborne—Wild Delight	7	12	4	Mr Raymond R. Guest Chocolate, pale blue hoops, armlets and cuffs, chocolate cap	D. L. Moore
111	2—ARKLE	B g by Archive—Bright Cherry	6	12	4	Anne Duchess of Westminster Yellow, black cap gold tassel	Dreaper
110	3—BEN STACK	B g by Tangle—Sweet Vernal	6	12	4	Ann Duchess of Westmin... Yellow, black cap, gold tassel	
110	4—SILVER GREEN	Gr g by High Ender—Maytime Glor...					
003	5—CHELSEA SET	B g by Artist's Son—Parry the Point					
033	6—WILLIE WAGTAIL III	Ch g by Snow King—Water Wagtail					
020	7—FERRY BOAT	Ch g by Buckhound—Boat Race					

The small figures in front of horses' numbers in...

FIFTH RACE

5.00 p.m.   2 m.

THE TICKELL STEEPLECHASE OF 500 SOVS, of which the second will receive 75 sovs and the third 50 sovs. Professional riders of the first three horses will receive £25, £15, £10 respectively. A handicap steeplechase for five years old and upwards. In making this handicap the Handicapper will start allotting the weights which he considers any horse at 9st 7lb and when he gets up to 12st 7lb will eliminate from the handicap all horses which he considers any horse at 9st 7lb and when he gets up to 12st 7lb. The names of these horses will not be published and they will not be charged any entrance fee. The winner of a steeplechase after publication of the weights (5th April, 10 a.m.) to carry 4lb extra; of a steeplechase value 525 sovs, 10lb extra; of a steeplechase value 400 sovs or steeplechases collectively value 800 sovs, 12lb extra. Riders—Confined to Professional Jockeys and Qualified Riders under I.N.H.S. Rules who have not ridden ten winners under any recognised Rules of Steeplechasing including Hurdle or Flat Races in which amateur riders were permitted to ride. Riders who have not ridden a winner allowed 3lb. No claim for allowances under Rule 45 (i).

ABOUT TWO MILES OVER THE BUSH FENCE COURSE

Rider			age	st	lb		Trainer
010	1—GREATRAKES	B g by Cacador—First Quarter	a	12 0 (in 4lb ex)		Mr R. J. McGrath Terra-cotta, yellow sash, purple cap	Private
100	2—BAXIPP...	...ER	a	11 13		Lord Fermoy Black, black cap, yellow hoop	A. S. O'Brien
			a	11 11		Mr J. F. Hoey Royal blue and cerise stripes, cerise slvs and cap	Hoey
			a	11 2		Mr J. G. Bredin Royal blue, white hoops, white cap, Royal blue spots	Bredin
			a	11 0		Mrs Frank Warren Dark purple, emerald green slvs, old gold cap	Warren
			a	10 10		Mr R. R. Clarke Maroon and turquoise qtd, maroon cap	W. E. Rooney
			a	10 9		Mrs D. J. Morgan Red, white spots	D. J. Morgan
			a	10 9		Mr John B. Ryan Green, pink collar and cuffs, pink cap, green hoop	Norris
			a	10 7		Mr D. Boyd Royal blue, white slvs and sash, Royal blue cap	Private
			a	10 7		Mr B. J. Ryan Dove grey and scarlet hoops, dove grey cap	M. Browne
			a	10 4		Mr A. J. Stark Bronze and yellow hlvd, hooped cap	D. Quirke
			a	10 4		Mrs Guy Shorrock Black, harlequin slvs, black cap	McCreery
						Miss Helen Bryce-Smith Pink, chocolate hooped cap	Bryce-...
						Mr A. L. Moore Chocolate, light blue slvs, chocolate cap, light blue hoop	D. L. Moore
						Mr L. G. Doyle Grey, wine slvs, wine cap, grey hoop	Private
						Mr Alec Watson ...lue, green slvs, black cap	Woods
						J. J. Nugent ...ocolate and white hlvd, ...d cap	Gleeson

...ings from 1st Jan. 1962

SECOND DAY

WEDNESDAY, MAY 1st, 1963

KILDARE AND NATIONAL HUNT STEEPLECHASES

PUNCHESTOWN

CONYNGHAM CUP

JOHN JAMESON

Perpetual Challenge Cup

PRICE ONE SHILLING

NO CARD AUTHENTIC UNLESS SIGNED

GREAT HORSES FROM MILL HOUSE TO ARKLE AND CHAMPION SUPREME ISTABRAQ

Glance back down the list of great horses that have graced the Punchestown scene and you discover immediately names that figure automatically in any compilation of the most charismatic performers in National Hunt history.

From Arkle to Istabraq, we bridge a span of almost 40 years and yet as we advance into the new Millennium, it is abundantly clear that when people read the 150 years long story of the Punchestown course, they will never be able to overlook that these were but two of the all-time greats that entered the winner's enclosure.

Pat Taaffe on the peerless Arkle who won the Jameson Cup at Punchestown '63, a year before he recorded the first of the three successive Cheltenham Gold Cup.

The Punchestown 'card from that day in 1963 when Arkle won the John Jameson Cup.

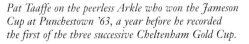

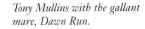

Tony Mullins with the gallant mare, Dawn Run.

*The then president,
Dr P.J. Hillary (centre)
pictured with Vincent O'Brien
and his brother Phonsie (right)
in the Committee Room
of Punchestown on the day
of the Great Match between
Dawn Run and Buck House
in April, 1986.*

It was fitting that as the 20th. century came to a close that Istabraq should have participated in the inaugural running of the £110,000 (Grade 1) Shell Champion Hurdle on the fourth day of the first four-day Festival meeting. Naturally, many who had not managed to get to Cheltenham to see him winning his second successive crown were now afforded the opportunity of acclaiming him.

And how the crowd loved it. They were 12 deep around the parade ring and the cheers reached a crescendo after the champion returned to the No. 1 spot, where Charlie Swan entered into the spirit of the occasion by firing his whip into the air.

Sporting owner, J.P. McManus had done Punchestown proud by allowing the dual champion to take his place in the field. It unquestionably guaranteed the success of the fourth day and swelled the attendance far beyond what might otherwise have been expected. That Istabraq should give another clinical display as victory was comfortably achieved at odds of 1/4 with three-and-a-half lengths to spare over English challenger

Decoupage was incidental. His very presence alone was enough in itself and that 1999 victory will be remembered with even more pleasure in years to come as it is set beside Istabraq taking the Smurfit Champion Hurdle for a third successive year at Cheltenham 2000, joining Hatton's Grace (1949-'87), Sir Ken (1952-'54), Persian War (1968-'70) and See You Then (1985-'87) as the only others to complete the three-timer since the Second World War.

And, of course, one can never forget the Great Match at Punchestown on April 23rd. 1986 between Dawn Run and Buck House that really caught the imagination of the public. It resulted in the gallant mare, Dawn Run who earlier had won the Cheltenham Gold Cup in the hands of Jonjo O'Neill - a victory incidentally that created scenes of over-flowing enthusiasm and emotion in the winner's enclosure that will never be forgotten - coming out on top in a fascinating battle before a packed attendance that included then President, Dr. P. J. Hillery.

A year before he won the first of three successive Cheltenham Gold Cups and came to be acknowledged as perhaps the greatest chaser of all time, Arkle won the John Jameson Cup of '63. The reputation of Tom Dreaper's charge was already such that he had only two opponents and one serious rival, the previous season's Champion Novice Hurdle winner, Silver Green to which he had to concede 8 lbs. The betting suggested no contest and Pat Taaffe romped away with the spoils in the already famous yellow and black colours of Anne Duchess of Westminster.

The first running in 1961 of the Martin Mahony Champion Novice Hurdle was, with the benefit of hindsight, a race of pronounced significance. Fred Winter came over to ride the four-year-old Anzio for Fulke Walwyn. Anzio could finish only fourth behind Danny St. J. Gough's rank outsider Gleniry (ridden by J. Devine), Moonsun and Flaming Page, beaten a total of thirteen lengths.

Mill House Falls

Two of the 19 runners fell, one of them Mill House, a mere four-year-old, if a strapping one, fulfilled Dave Dick's prophecy by winning the 1963 Gold Cup for the same jockey-trainer combination.

Following the Martin Mahony Champion Novice Hurdle of 1961, he had been bought from breeder Mrs. Bridget Lawlor of Naas by the legendary bloodstock agent Jack Doyle - perhaps one of the greatest pieces of judgement ever - for English owner Bill Gollings as a potential Gold Cup winner. Mill House at first went to be trained by Syd Dale at Epsom, but later was transferred to Walwyn's yard at Lambourn.

It is history now how Mill House, regarded as unbeatable by his trainer, failed to Arkle in that epic clash between them in the 1964 Gold Cup and in time Fulke Walwyn was forced to admit: "Arkle broke the great horse's heart".

And to think that in both their cases, they had graced the Punchestown scene...

We have seen already how Workman (1939) and Lovely Cottage (1946), both winners of the Aintree Grand National were two other notable chasers that tested their prowess over the Punchestown obstacles. Lovely Cottage had won the Conyngham in 1944. Lough Conn was a great favourite with the Punchestown crowd, and he was runner-up in a field of 57 to 100/1 shot Lovely Cottage in the 1947 Aintree Grand National.

Nowadays, many of the finest hurdlers and chasers - quite a few of whom are seeking to follow up on Cheltenham success or make amends for failure there - participate for rich prizes at Punchestown with its bush fences . In 1999 Anzum which had narrowly beaten J.P. McManus's Le Coudray in the Stayers' Hurdle at Cheltenham won the Ballymore Properties Champion Stayers Hurdle for David 'The Duke' Nicholson at 7/1 as Le Coudray was installed 1/2 favourite. And the Nicky Henderson-trained Katarino who had been so highly-impressive in winning the Triumph Hurdle at Cheltenham confirmed the form by taking the I.A.W.S. Champion Hurdle.

The ill-fated Cardinal Hill, rated unlucky by his trainer Noel Meade at Cheltenham, made ample amends by winning the County Pride Champion Novice Hurdle.

But perhaps the most popular success of all over the four days was that of Imperial Call in the Heineken Gold Cup, as he floored the odds of 4/7 laid on Florida Pearl with Dorans Pride filling third position.

The greatest memory that I carried away with me from Punchestown '99 was of that victory of Imperial Call on the Wednesday and the scenes that followed in the winner's enclosure.

In a way they were a throw-back to the day in 1996 at Cheltenham when Imperial Call won the Gold Cup and hundreds of Cork enthusiasts who flooded into the winner's enclosure gave us an unforgettable rendering of "The Banks Of My Own Lovely Lee", as they unfurled a banner with the words "IMPERIAL CALL" on it and waved their mini-Tricolours.

Fergie Sutherland had been the hero of the hour that day. Now, although retired from training, he was there for the moment when Ruby Walsh came back in on 'Imperial' to a thunderous reception.

Fergie, for whom it was vindication in a way, was showered with good wishes by those who did not forget at that moment his contribution to providing such a red-letter day at Cheltenham '96. And he loved it all.

Now the day belonged to Ruby Walsh, who punched the air in delight as the 10-year-old passed the post after running his rivals ragged. And it belonged also to Raymond Hurley, who took over from Fergie Sutherland when he called it a day the previous summer.

The 23-year-old trainer was justifiably thrilled - and very proud- after the race. "It was great to see Imperial Call redeeming himself like that after all he had been through."

A victory smile from Tony Mullins in the winner's enclosure as he shares an unforgettable moment with John Clarke and owner Mrs. Charmian Hill.

The Great Match
Memorable Clash between Dawn Run and Buck House

I wasn't at Cheltenham when Arkle won his first Gold Cup in 1964 but of all the memories I retain from the period of over twenty years that I have been going there, few, if any, can ever match the manner in which Jonjo O'Neill snatched victory from the jaws of defeat in the 1986 Gold Cup. It ranks with the most thrilling and dramatic races of all for the Blue Riband of chasing. The overall impact can never fade from the memory.

The same year, Mrs. Seamus Purcell's Buck House, trained by Mouse Morris, was the brilliant winner of the Queen Mother Champion Chase.

These two victories then formed the prelude to what became known as the Great Match between them at Punchestown on April 23rd, '86.

Plans to bring the two outstanding horses into opposition in a championship race at Gowran Park folded, but Mrs. Purcell's husband, along with the Coolmore Stud, the Punchestown Racecourse and the Racing Board, put together £25,000 to tempt Mrs. Charmian Hill into allowing Dawn Run to meet Buck House over his best trip, two miles ten furlongs shorter than that of the Gold Cup.

A Tall Order

It looked a tall order for Dawn Run who was to meet her rival at level weights, without the sex allowance which many thought had just swung the balance in her favour at Cheltenham. Mrs. Hill nonetheless consented, and despite criticism of the Racing Board's contribution of £10,000 to an event in which only two owners were involved, it proved a huge success.

A Great Day for National Hunt Racing

Perhaps an element of uncertainty was added by reason of Dawn Run's post-Cheltenham fall at the first fence of Liverpool's Whitbread Gold Lable Cup Chase. More likely the mare's popularity, her reunion with Tony Mullins and the brilliance of Buck House were greater incentives. Whatever the reason, the enclosures were packed long before the race,

MEMORABLE CLASH BETWEEN DAWN RUN AND BUCK HOUSE AT PUNCHESTOWN... Buck House (Tommy Carmody) left and Dawn Run (Tony Mullins) right jumping the last ditch in the Great Match at Punchestown on April 23rd 1986, that really caught the imagination of the public.

Tony Mullins, Tommy Carmody and Paddy Mullins talking it over after the excitement generated by the Great Match had finished.

and as the two horses, produced in splendid condition by Paddy Mullins and Mouse Morris, made their way to the start, the stands were packed, spectators hung from every vantage point - and Vincent O'Brien had been tempted from his Ballydoyle base to make a rare appearance at a N.H. meeting.

Not Much In It

Despite the conditions of the event Dawn Run was favourite, but there was not much in it, 4/6 as against 11/8, and any notion that this would be an exhibition round was soon dispelled. Tommy Carmody on Buck House, never let Dawn Run out of his sights. He constantly harried her and threw down the gauntlet racing to the third last fence. A marvellous jump gave Buck House a clear advantage for the first time, to a roar of approval from his supporters. He increased the lead at the tricky second last fence and faced up to the last with a margin that, against a less dogged opponent, would have entitled him to be hailed the winner.

Renewed Effort

Tony Mullins asked Dawn Run for a renewed effort. As if sensing she had to atone for her Liverpool lapse, she quickened instantly, was in front rising to the final fence, and even though jumping to the left, scampered home by 2.5 lengths.

The reception she received, and Buck House also, almost rivalled the scenes at Cheltenham. It was a great day for National Hunt Racing in general and Tony Mullins in particular for he had lost the rides on the mare in both the Champion Hurdle and Gold Cup.

But what tragedies the following months were to bring to the connections of both horses. Dawn Run was killed contesting the Grande Course de Haies d'Auteuil, taking a terrible fall and breaking her neck. That was on 27 June - and Buck House was already dead three weeks, having succumbed to a colic out in a paddock.

How fortunate we were to see them at Punchestown on a never-to-be-forgotten Spring day in 1986 in that inspired match.

9

CONTROVERSY STEMMED FROM INTRODUCTION OF BUSH COURSE IN 1960

The introduction of the bush fence course to Punchestown in 1960 did not happen without a deal of controversy. Indeed, it aroused deep passion and intense debate between what one might term the 'traditionalists' and the advocates of change.

Major John de Burgh, who numbered himself among those who felt that change was inevitable if Punchestown was to keep pace with modern developments in the National Hunt sphere, said he never for one moment doubted the sincerity of the 'traditionalists'. Their thinking was based on the fact that the move away from the banks and stone wall would represent the death of Punchestown as it had come into being in 1850 and the death also of all the traditions - and the legends - that had come to be associated directly with races over these type of obstacles.

Other courses, they argued, could change but what Punchestown had was something that was sacrosanct and which gave it a uniqueness that put it on a pedestal apart.

Major de Burgh recalls a famous meeting in the Courthouse Building in Naas where matters came to a head. In the course of his speech to the packed audience in favour of change, he ended by saying that any reasonable man would have to accept the arguments as he had outlined them. Someone stood up at the back of the hall and exclaimed: "When you say any 'reasonable man', you mean anyone who agrees with you!"

Frank O'Reilly, whose association with Punchestown goes back a long time, watches as a bush fence is prepared for the Spring Festival meeting. Also in the photograph is Mrs. Joan Moore, Secretary/Manager of Punchestown.

But the advocates of change won the day - and Punchestown never looked back.

Major de Burgh, as one who had ridden with distinction himself, said that as a result of the impact made by Irish-bred and Irish-trained horses since the end of the Second World War, overseas buyers with the money to spend were looking more and more to this country for the type of horse that they believed could go on to reach the top of the ladder in the National Hunt sphere. They hadn't to be reminded of Prince Regent (1946), Cottage Rake (1948-'50) and Knock Hard (1953) landing five Gold Cups between them awhile Early Mist (1953), Royal Tom (1954) and Quare Times (1955) won three successsive Aintree Grand nationals to add to Caughoo's triumph in 1947.

Major de Burgh pointed out that a horse could injure a joint at the stone wall that would put it out maybe for months or even end its career prematurely. Thus a valuable sale would be lost, especially if it was a chaser with a lot of potential.

While the 'traditionalists' could argue that Workman and Lovely Cottage were among winners of the Aintree Grand National who had impressed at Punchestown it could not be denied that a majority of owners and trainers were increasingly reluctant to risk valuable thoroughbred horses over the banks and stone wall obstacles.

It was significant that none of Vincent O'Brien's stars had taken that road to either Cheltenham or Liverpool, nor indeed Tom Dreaper's Prince Regent, and this famous venue would not have seen chasers of the class of Arkle, Dawn Run and Buck House, or the promotion of international racing, had not the change been made.

In 1961, a new course allowed hurdle races to be run for the first time on this hallowed turf and it was not long before the inevitable happened - the running of a Bumpers race. Later still came flat racing.

Giving it that final touch with the clippers in front of an appreciative audience.

The bush fences and hurdles were an immediate hit at Punchestown. Despite the fixture's late date, there was an immediate jump in the class of runner and, from the outset, there was support from British trainers, whose participation of course increased quite dramatically during the Nineties.

With its ditches, banks and walls, the old Punchestown dating back to 1850 was an unique course but one that time was leaving behind. The days were passing when a small farmer kept a brood mare 'with a bit of blood' in the hopes of rearing from her a horse that would graduate to Punchestown, via the hunting field and the point-to-point. A horse that would win or at least run well at the Kildare venue before eventually becoming hard cash in the breeder's pocket.

The small farmer-bloodstock breeder would inevitably, of course, remain an integral - and essential part of the breeding scene - but now 'his bit of blood' never saw a hunting field in her life and her offspring became destined (the farmer hoped) to fetch a tidy price, as a yearling, from an owner interested in acquiring the makings of a good money-spinning performer.

The business of 'chaser building' if one might term it thus had become more specialised. The budding jumper made his debut in a bumper, then ran over hurdles before graduating to the bigger obstacles. He was seldom if ever schooled over banks and walls the obstacles typical of Punchestown.

Building a fence with expert knowledge that will test a chasers prowess.

BUT THE DOUBLE BANK AND STONE WALL REMAINED A FEATURE OF PUNCHESTOWN... The Double Bank still remains a feature of certain races at Punchestown to-day. Here Digacre (Andrew McNamara), No 6. is pictured on his way to victory from Tearaway King (Enda Bolger), at Punchestown in the Ernest & Young Chase for the Ladies Perpetual Cup.

Up to 1960, when the bush course was introduced, if such a horse became a reasonably good, or very good, chaser he never bid for Punchestown prizes but was confined to orthodox fences. In a sense a pity, but the natural outcome of a policy dictated harshly by finance.

Changed All That

The new bush course changed everything overnight. It brought a new and welcome meaning to Punchestown. No one wanted to do away with the fundamental function of Punchestown - the meeting where the hunter-chaser came into his own on a course specially fitted to permit him to reveal bold, cat-like jumping and initiative in negotiating varied and natural obstacles - the unique characteristics of the Irish hunter.

Bush fences lent variety to Punchestown. It meant that, along with the best of the hunter-chasers, the public could see other steeplechasers, who had made their mark in this country and across the water, in action against each other.

However, the new changes did not mean that the old features were completely eliminated. A number of them, including the famous double and the stone wall, remained. One could not visualise Punchestown without these obstacles because they catered for a certain type of performer. And Punchestown by its very traditions catered for them in a very special way.

Balance Achieved

So those who loved to watch a race over banks continued to do so. A balance was achieved that was admirable. The Punchestown Management Committee deserved a great deal of credit for its courage and foresight at the time.

As we have seen, the bush fences and hurdles were an immediate hit and there was an immediate jump in the class of runner.

The stone wall was also retained and this picture from 1997 shows the winner Tearaway King (Enda Bolger), on inside, jumping the obstacle with Dennistown Thriller (Philip Fenton) and Thamer's Run (Andrew Coonan), both next to him.

Sponsors were more easily attracted to support the races over the bush course. New life was given to the meeting and trainers were willing now to run that type of performer, the "park chaser" which could not have been seen in action at the old Punchestown.

By the year 2000 the passions that had been engendered during the famous meeting in the Courthouse Building in Naas might seem difficult for the younger generation to comprehend. But, as Major John de Burgh stressed, the 'traditionalists' were totally sincere in their outlook and, not alone saw it as something akin to sacrilege to break with tradition but even viewed the modernising of Punchestown as sounding the death-knell of one of the oldest fixtures in the Irish racing calendar.

I wonder if some of those same 'traditionalists' who have passed on were present for the 150th anniversary Festival meeting of 2000 would they be as passionate now as they were on that famous occasion in the Courthouse Building in Naas.

Or would mature acceptance have come with the passage of close on forty years?

10

BRIDGET LAWLOR –
'THE HEROINE OF PUNCHESTOWN'

Con Costello

The finest accolade they could pay her was to describe her as 'the heroine of Punchestown'.

Yes, Mrs. Bridget Lawlor, who in her prime thought nothing of catering for up to 10,000 people without a hitch. Not alone did her business, from its Naas base, provide the catering at Punchestown but also for the Kildare Hunt Ball when it was still held in Naas Town Hall.

She was seen as 'a genius in her organisation, like a general directing her staff, her history an epic of food and drink'. Even in her later years, when confined to bed, she still directed operations by telephone.

She provided casual work for many in the County Kildare area
that was highly valued in lean times, especially during the days
of The Emergency. The major part of the work force, however,
came from Naas town and district.

*Mrs. Bridget Lawlor in old age surrounded by her
grandchildren as she happily reads a story to them*

Her workforce came mainly from Naas Town and district- and those engaged valued it highly in lean times

To-day many of those workers still talk about their outdoor catering years with nostalgia. One woman in her eighties recalls going to work for Mrs. Lawlor at the age of fourteen, buttering sandwiches. Then the cooking was done on open fires, and the first job of the day on arrival at a venue was to light the fires and prepare for the cooking. The advent of bottled gas for cooking was hailed by the workers as a miracle. The staff was always fed before the serving of the food commenced. All of the food used was fresh, and the preparation and cooking for thousands of customers was undertaken in an organised way. Linen table cloths and napkins together with fresh flowers always enhanced the tables.

If outdoor catering events, such as Galway Races, extended over a number of days, the women collected bags of straw and slept in a hut at the racecourse. But normally when a function was over and the washing up and packing was done, the women climbed into the lorries to take up their seats on the butter boxes for the journey home.

To pass the time, they sang together but as they came near to Naas they grew silent, thinking of their families at home, and hoping that all was well. They would also know that when they got back to Naas that the hampers of surplus food would be distributed to them according to their needs as Mrs. Lawlor would have given the supervisor a list of recipients. She was as professional in her staff relations as she was in management. Even the redoubtable parish priest Fr. P.J. Doyle speaking from the pulpit on the feast of St. Brigid reminded his flock that they had their own St. Bridget just across the road!

In 1944, a year before the Second World War ended, a journalist wrote: 'At Old Mill House lives a lady who knows more than most about food. A Punchestown heroine if ever there was one, for she was born on the spot and the races still run over part of her brother's land.'

Legendary Bloodstock agent, the late Jack Doyle who sold Mill House for Mrs. Lawlor to English owner, Bill Gollings.

One can appreciate then her affinity with the course and especially with the Spring Festival meeting. She bred and sold a number of outstanding horses in the National Hunt sphere including the great Mill House who won the Cheltenham Gold Cup of 1963 for W.H. Gollings and figured in the 1964 epic with Arkle for the Blue Riband of chasing and whose major successes included the Hennessy Gold Cup in 1963 and '67.

Other notable horses that passed through her hands were Bawnogues and Nás na Riogh. The Keely farm at Bawnoge, Punchestown, where Bridget Lawlor was born, was visited by Lord Walter FitzGerald in 1905: he called there to see the granite cross from Ballyknocken which had recently been erected in response to a request from the priest of Ballymore Eustace who had blessed the cattle when one had collapsed and appeared to be dying. If the cross were erected, the priest said, no more cattle would be afflicted.

As a young woman, Bridget Keely went to work at Palmerstown, and from there she married Myles Lawlor from Lacken and they went to live on a 16 acre farm at Greenhills, Kill, where their sons Jim and Tom were born. When she opened her restaurant, and later the hotel and ballroom (at Corban's Mill) they went to live in the Mill House. That residence was to provide the name for her successful Mill House.

In 1913 she opened a small restaurant at Poplar Square, Naas. A few months later she began to do a little outdoor catering, and this flourished so unexpectedly that she was obliged to extend her premises. Her really first important contract was that for the Co. Kildare Hunt Club Ball, and after that came Punchestown.

In 1930 a ballroom was opened which became the popular venue for annual Hunt Balls and functions held by such groups as the Garda, farmers and milk producers. In 1913 the restaurant was given the imprimatur of quality when Lady Mayo from Palmerstown and her friend Sir James Power of John's Lane Distillery went to dine there.

The dining-room and bar have retained their high standards to this day. The accommodation side of the business was closed some years ago.

During the depression of the 1920's and 1930's when even the pubs did bad business, Mrs. Lawlor remembered the support given to her by Sir James Power and consequently arranged that only Powers whiskey was sold at all of her outlets!

Bridget Lawlor was a legend in her lifetime. Single handedly, and without any formal training in her sphere, she developed her establishment from being a small town restaurant to one which was synonymous with that of Naas to thousands of travellers on the main road from the south. A halt at Lawlors became an integral part of the annual journey to Croke Park.

But Mrs. Lawlor was to become even more nationally famous when she undertook the complicated contracts for outdoor catering. Having acquired a bar licence in 1922 she catered for the Kildare Hunt Club Ball in Naas Town Hall that year. In time she was to provide suppers for the Tipperary, West Waterford, Thurles & Kilshane, Bray, Longford, Limerick, Kilmoganny, Westmeath and Johnswell Hunt Balls.

By 1931 she could advertise in the official programme for the Royal Dublin Society bi-centenary commemoration, that she catered for not only the RDS, but also for race meetings at Punchestown, Naas, Mullingar, Dundalk, Thurles and Gowran Park, as well as at major functions in Maynooth, Clongowes Wood and Knockbeg Colleges, and for the Royal Irish Automobile Club and the Irish International Grand Prix in the Phoenix Park, Dublin. In 1932 she was amongst the caterers who fed the multitudes at the Eucharistic Congress, also held in the Phoenix Park.

Nas Na Riogh winning the Blessington Cup at Punchestown 1952 for Mrs. Lawlor with Pat Taaffe in the saddle.

At Christmas time Mrs. Lawlor hosted great parties for the children of her friends in the ballroom, but to many more people, the ballroom is nostagically remembered for the Sunday night dances and the Balls. The Hunt Balls, for which the walls were decorated with murals depicting the hung; the Farmers' and Garda Dances to the big band sounds of Mick Delahunty and Jummy Dunny were great annual social events.

acquaintance with soup had been to get it in a bowl with half a dozen potatoes and a lump of meat.

To him, soup was nothing but the water the meat had been boiled in. He took one look at the plate of consomme and made for the door. 'Don't you like your soup, sir?' The waitress asked him. 'You may take it away.'said Dunne with spirit. 'let them that ate the meat drink the soup'. From the minute that story got around he was never called anything but Soup Dunne'.

A decade later in an American magazine Maura Laverty again wrote about Mrs. Lawlor, 'the most considerable employer in Naas, whose business acumen and hard work had changed an unpretentious village boarding-house into the largest family catering business in Europe. Her tastes remain as simple as when, nearly forty years ago, she laid the cornerstone of a great enterprise by serving teas at Naas sports meetings. Last Horse Show Week she served 38,850 luncheons and 31,630 teas.

Bridget Lawlor passed away in 1969. She was succeeded by her son Tom who died in 1975. His wife Helen and son Tom then ran the business up to the time it was sold in the last two years to Louis Fitzgerald of the Poitin Stil.

Maura Laverty, the Rathangan writer, was familiar with the hotel in the 1940's and included a mention of it in her novel More Than Human (1944). 'Soup Dunne was a farmer who belonged to one of the richest families in Ballyderrig, people who for all their money had a very poor way of living. He was at Naas fair one day when he decided to treat himself to dinner in Mrs. Lawler's (sic) new eating-house. He had never seen the like of it, waitresses with caps, and flowers on the table and all. A plate of lovely clear soup was put before him. Now Dunne's only previous

11

NOTED FAMILIES CARRIED ON PUNCHESTOWN'S PROUD TRADITIONS

Raymond Smith

What fascinates the historian most of all about Punchestown as it celebrates its 150th birthday is the manner in which its proud traditions have been carried on down the decades by certain noted families.

Names that automatically spring to mind are the Moores, the Beasleys, the Floods, the Dreapers, the Hartys, the Osbornes, the Taaffes and, of course, the Mullins family of Goresbridge, County Kilkenny.

Sons followed fathers in riding the course and derived immense satisfaction in entering the winner's enclosure during the Spring Festival meeting. In quite a few instances they in turn took up training and it seemed incumbent on them that they should have a winner to their name at this track. The cycle always seemed to turn full circle and renew itself.

MAJOR JOHN de BURGH... his family won the Kildare Hunt Cup with Medora in 1850 the first year of Punchestown as we know it to-day.

Hubert de Burgh pictured in 1924.

The Governor General's Cup won by Hubert de Burgh at Punchestown in the 1930's.

Others who may not have been prominent riders or trainers were deeply involved with the Kildare Hunt and this in turn led them to an involvement with the progress and advancement of the interests of the racecourse itself. Their time, of course was given on a purely voluntary basis.

Reading back through the records, one cannot but be struck by some of the amazing characters connected with Punchestown. Judging by their audacious exploits, some of these individuals could merit a book on their own. It seemed as if success in life measured strictly in monetary terms and adherence to the standards of normal behaviour would have represented a slow death to them. They had to live constantly on the high wire. And if they paid a hard price in the end, they were so beloved by those who knew them and shared their *joie de vivre* that they were paid overwhelming funeral tributes as they passed to the Great Beyond.

John Maher of Castlewarden, where he maintained a pack of hounds, certainly ranked among those sportsmen who enjoyed the high life. He also kept a blind piper who played to his guests after dinner and retained an artist on the premises, who painted only one subject i.e. a sailor saved from a shipwreck in Dublin Bay and sitting on a rock.

He had the habit as related in the book A History of the Kildare Hunt, of making his huntsman leap over a high gate with a half crown between each knee and the saddle, as a means of keeping him to the required standard. The man was suitably admonished if in the act of leaping he let fall either of the coins.

John Maher ended his life in Naas Gaol as a hopeless debtor. During his prison years, he enjoyed the companionship of George Sidwell, whose affairs were in a similar unfortunate position. Both inmates made the best of their circumstances in Naas Gaol, then under the genial governorship of Captain Woodruff, and spent what little money they could scrape together in sending out for "something" to cheer their drooping spirits.

John Maher's father Gilbert, a man of some substance in County Tipperary never made any effort to release his ne'er-do-well son. It was a distinct saving of money to keep him in Naas Gaol instead of at Castlewarden. But when he died he was accorded a noble funeral and today he lies with his forefathers in County Tipperary.

The two families extant that go right back to the very origins of Punchestown are the de Burghs and the de Robecks.

We find that Thomas John de Burgh had the distinction on the first of April 1850 - the year from which we date the Punchestown of today - of winning the Kildare Hunt Cup with his own mare Medora which he rode himself.

The race was confined to members of the Kildare Hunt and was run over a three-mile course with each of the contestants carrying 12 st.

Thomas John de Burgh was Chairman of the Hunt in his day and owned a number of good horses. There is a link through marriage between them. In 1878 Emily, daughter of the 4th Baron married Lt. Col Thomas de Burgh of Oldtown.

That same Lt. Col Thomas John de Burgh was grandfather of Major John Hubert de Burgh, who, not surprisingly, had racing and a love of horses and riding bred in his veins.

In the study of Oldtown Stud at Oldtown, Naas, he recalled the era when the members of certain families were spurred by the maxim that you had to be a good shot, follow the hunt with enthusiasm and fight a good war.

Hubie de Burgh who is to-day Managing Director of the Derrinstown Stud pictured at the yearling sales at Goffs in 1998 with Angus Gold.

Fair Salina bred at Major John de Burgh's Oldtown Stud, Naas who won the Epsom Oaks, Irish Oaks, and Yorkshire Oaks, in 1975.

Thus it was taken for granted that the men should go off to war in days before this country got its independence. Major John de Burgh took part in the North African campaign during the Second World War and in the invasion of Italy. Later when the War ended he was stationed for a number of years in Germany. He smiled when he recalled that he was the champion rider in both Germany and Austria but added modestly, that it was only to be expected as the Army could provide the best horses.

In Britain, he made his name as an outstanding amateur over a three-year period and was associated with the legendary Ivor Anthony. He rode at all the National Hunt tracks around the country but did not have the pleasure of riding a winner at Cheltenham.

On his return to Ireland he got very much involved on the Punchestown Committee and admits that matters did no always go smoothly. The biggest crisis was when the moment of decision came to introduce the bush fences in 1960.

He recalled being brought to Punchestown for the first time when he was only five and the wonder of it all. There were just two top National Hunt courses in the country then - Fairyhouse and Punchestown - and, of course, the Punchestown Spring Festival meeting was THE great occasion of the year.

He remembers that there were natural, indeed brilliant jumpers, of the big banks. A handful could, literally skip over the double bank. He recalled a keen enthusiast arriving from Britain for the meeting one year and being simply amazed when he timed with his stop-watch how fast one of the races was run.

Major de Burgh remembered a man called Willie Farrell bringing a mare all the way from Clare to Punchestown and going for a 'touch'. He lost everything he had and never went back home. "He remained on working here on our farm. He always wore a bowler hat to church - to everything. It became a part of him".

The 7th Baron Martin de Robeck pictured with his wife Caroline at the last Kildare Hunt Ball in Castletown House.

Baroness Caroline de Robeck sat in the study of Gowran Grange, Co. Kildare in front of a blazing fire and enumerated for me in fascinating fashion how the family came originally from Sweden to this country - and of its long links with the Kildare Hunt. Her late husband Martin (the 7th Baron) was very involved with Punchestown racecourse, more particularly in the equestrian field.

One of the earliest Barons - the second - who had distinguished service in the Swedish Army had the good fortune - or rather one might say misfortune - to fall in love with the same girl as the future King of Sweden. "You could hardly be a rival in love for the hand of the girl that the King wanted for himself", said the Baroness with a smile.

So he departed Sweden and, after various adventures in different countries, (including having a horse shot under him in one famous Battle in the mid-18th Century) eventually settled in Ireland. The reason why the de Robeck family seat was called

Gowran Grange was that John Henry Fock, the 2nd Baron married Anne, sole heiress of the Hon Richard Fitzpatrick. The land stretched at one stage from Blanchardstown to County Kilkenny.

Back in the mid-19th century, it seemed automatic for each Baron de Robeck in turn to become Master of the Kildare Hunt. Reading through *A History Of The Kildare Hunt*, which was published in 1913 and is now a collector's item, one gets a clear insight into the tremendous contribution the family made to the development and well-being of the Hunt.

The vacancy caused by the resignation of Lord Naas in the Spring of 1862 saw the then Baron de Robeck succeed him as the unanimous choice of the members. "Baron de Robeck's family had been long and honourably known in Kildare", wrote the joint authors of the book, the Earl of Mayo and W.B. Boulton. "Baron de Robeck himself, as appears from notes from his own diary, had regularly hunted with the Kildares since the year 1853. It was felt in the county that no better sportsman could have been found to succeed Lord Naas and that a continuance of the good sport and

John the 4th Baron de Robeck.

Martin de Robeck helping in the design of the Three-Day Event course at Punchestown in the early seventies.

general prosperity which had attended the late Mastership was likely to be maintained under his auspices. Those anticipations were abundantly realised during the six seasons that followed." Fulsome praise indeed...

All For The Hounds

The 5th Baron de Robeck bankrupted himself in order to ensure that he would have a pack of hounds befitting the Hunt. "I think things became so bad in the end that his wife and children left him and he was down to one table and chair. He had only one handkerchief for the top pocket of his coat which he would wash every night so that it would look spotless the next day", the Baroness told me.

The tradition of steeplechasing can be traced back in this country to its origin at the local hunt meetings. And in time Punchestown, as we know it today, grew out of the Kildare Hunt, who actually owned the lands which eventually became the permanent course for the great Spring meeting.

Modest Meetings

There is little doubt that early in the 19th century it was the custom of members of the Kildare Hunt to improvise some modest little meetings at which gentlemen and farmers alike could indulge their taste of riding over a typical bit of Kildare country-side. These early meetings were held at various venues other than Punchestown. There is a record of one being held at the back of the ruins of Jigginstown Castle, a little off the main road about half-a-mile outside Naas town.

Amazingly enough, they had erected a couple of "ill-constructed stands on which we did not choose to risk our precious carcasses", wrote one observer who went on to describe the line of tents stretching from east to west of the course and in which many a rustic couple figured away in reels and jigs, and hornpipes to the well-known airs of 'Shiver The Quilt', 'Father Jack Walsh', 'My duck's in the house' and 'The Night of the Win'.

THE BARON WHO GAVE ALL FOR HIS PACK... the 5th Baron de Robeck who went bankrupt to ensure that his Hunting pack was properly maintained.

A family gathering of the de Robecks outside Gowran Grange.

A meeting held in Kilcock in 1833 produced a doggerel poem that gave a rather interesting insight into what the gathering at a race meeting could be like at the time:

We'd many a stiff necked brat of a dandy
Lots of Parliament, poteen and brandy,
Carloads of nieces and country cousins
Jingles and old charabangs in dozens,
Bogtrotters, turfcutters, butchers and bakers,
Jackasses, parsons, a few undertakers;
Pawnbrokers pledging their honour and word;
Pickpockets found you wherever you stirred.
Some girls handsome and some girls shy
Whose names you shall have in print by and bye;
Country attorneys and country squireens,
Jarveys and donkeys and one horse machines;
Some people sober and some people drunk,
Unlucky gamesters in a hell of a funk.
Sugarstick, gingerbread not at all spiced,
Cripples on crutches, legs broken and spliced.
Crabapples and currants, cooks, cowboys and cods
The knowing coves giving and taking the odds.
These and of rum 'uns a very large stock
I met at the races last week at Kilcock.

The Marquess of Drogheda

One cannot write about the contributions of certain famous personalities and families to Punchestown without putting the spotlight on the Marquis of Drogheda, who came to to be known simply as "Mr. Punchestown". He became 'hooked' on Punchestown as young man when Westmeath, his favourite hunter, provided him with a winner at the Kildare Hunt Point to Point.

Westmeath, like all the subsequent winners in his colours, was trained by Michael Moneypenny at Moore Abbey in Monasterevin. In fact, Westmeath went on to win the Kildare Hunt Cup four times in five years from1849.

Tremendous Vision

The Marquis was a man of tremendous vision. Not Alone did he want to establish at Punchestown a fixture that would attract to Ireland in international clientele but that jump races would be conducted under their own particular rules and governed by an authority, a ruling body that would compliment rather than compete with the Turf Club.

In a remarkable four-year span from 1865, he saw all these dreams transformed into reality. His brainwave was adding the Conyngham Cup to the Punchestown programme.

THE MARQUESS OF DROGHEDA...
'hooked' on Punchestown as a young man.

It became one of the most prestigious events of all to him. The following year he was elected a Steward of the Turf Club for the first time and marked his new status by preparing of a comprehensive set of regulations under the title "The Irish National Hunt Steeplechase Rules". To enforce the new code he promoted the foundation of the Irish National Hunt Steeplechase Committee.

Was the Marquess There

On another plane he was determined to clean up Irish racing and a journalist of the time wrote that "he was both respected and feared and men who tried to play knavish tricks, with his eyes watching them from the Steward's Stand, played them to their cost." No wonder when news of big coups reached a wider audience, the first question set by the racing fan was a simple one - " Was the Marquis there?"

One of the big gambling attractions at Punchestown are invariably the bumpers and here too one sees the handiwork of the Marquis. The amateur status of these riders was laid down in 1877 and qualification opened up to a wider pool of horsemen as previously you had to be either a serving officer in the army or navy or belong to a select group of Clubs to take part.

A Family Tradition

The Grainger Family of Eadestown, Naas, can record well over a century of loyal employment at nearby Punchestown. Mick Grainger was the first of them to work there as foreman, a position which he held for 50 years. He could recall the race meetings before any of the stands were built. He was succeeded as foreman by his son Johnny, who also spent half a century working there, from 1879 to 1929. He died in 1963 at the age of 98. He was succeeded by his nephew Mick who was employed there for 47 years, and he in turn was followed by three of his nephews, brothers Jim, Dick and Marty Grainger. Jim recalls reporting for work there at the age of 14 in 1952, and he remained there for the next eighteen years. The faithfulness of the family to the steeplechase venue is remembered in the local saying that "there is always a Grainger at Punchestown".

Furthermore, in every race at the meeting his heritage is in evidence for he was the man who introduced numbered saddle cloths, an innovation he had seen on a trip to Australia.

He was serving his 26th year as a Steward of the Turf Club when he died on the eve of the 1892 Irish Derby and such had been his dominance that many believed the big race itself would have to be cancelled.

But it went ahead- and that is certainly the way he would have wanted it. Yes, a pillar of racing in his day, his lasting impact in Punchestown and Irish racing generally gives him a splendid place in this history and in the history of the Irish Turf.

The Martin Family

The Martin family played a major role in the management of Punchestown over a long number of years. When Peter Martin took over as Secretary/Manager in 1969, he was succeeding his father Capt. L.J. Martin, who had been very much involved in a change-over from a glorified Point-To-Point meeting to a high-class steeplechase and hurdle course. Peter himself would see the advent of Flat racing but he held the conviction that the chief role of Punchestown was to cater for the National Hunt racing and to maintain - and jealously guard - the tradition that was established as far back as 1850.

He had known a chequered career before he first became a Senior Judge to the Irish Turf Club in 1967, and then assumed the responsibilities that went with being Secretary/Manager at Punchestown.

His school days were spent at Downside but during the holidays he hunted regularly, before weight put a stop to it, and then he switched to the Point-To-Points.

He recalled "one wonderful season" when he hunted five days a week. My father was master of the North Kildare Harriers at the time and I hunted with the Harriers as well as with the Wards and the Meaths."

Peter Martin in retirement and his wife Anne take a relaxed view of their beloved course before Punchestown got under way and the new £8.75 million complex was providing patrons with the new modern amenity.

You might say that he saw the world after that before returning with his wife, Anne to Ireland in 1962 and becoming a Stewards Secretary to the Turf Club.

He spent three months in the West Indies before joining Lord Derby's Stanley House stable, working there for a season and chiefly learning about stud work. Then followed a spell at the Lambourn stables of Atty Perrse, finishing up as his assistant. Off then to the States o the famous Claborne Stud Farm in Kentucky, run by the renowned Ben Hancock. Peter Martin was there when Nasrullah was at the top of his form and the list of sires also included Bold Ruler and Round Table.

As far back as 1969 Peter Martin was able to see that Punchestown provided very inadequate facilities for its racegoers. He could see that the stands were old-fashioned and he went on record to state prophetically that "if you want to increase attendances at race meetings, you have to improve the facilities-and then go out and sell them to the public in a very positive way."

PETER MARTIN... in his days at the helm as Secretary Manager.

He had seen how the Americans went about promoting racing and while he realised that some of the ideas might not be practical for a country like ours, there was still a lot that could be done.

"Punchestown has tremendous local appeal." he said. "It brings out the grass roots of National Hunt racing. The small producer, for instance, still likes to keep his Point–To-Point horses for Punchestown. It is the culmination of the small man's dreams and this is something that will never change."

"Punchestown is a beautiful setting and occurs at a good-time of year. One really feels with the gorse in bloom and the girls dressed up that winter is at least over for another year."

Thirty years on from when he took over at the helm, Peter Martin had reason to be proud of the 'new Punchestown' because it was, in a way, the culmination of dreams he had of the need for new facilities back in 1969, but there was none of the money available then to start on the type of Development Programme that was initiated in 1997.

True, in his time came new Tote areas and a new stand and much improved catering facilities but there was no way that an all embracing £8.75 million complex could have been started from scratch and completed so quickly.

The private box was not in vogue as a means of raising finance. Other tracks - even Leopardstown, Fairyhouse, the Curragh and Galway were in the same boat.

The creation of the Irish Horseracing Authority and the financial backing provided by the Government for racecourse development plans changed the whole scenario overnight- and Punchestown was quick to move with the times.

Mrs. Joan Moore (left) who succeeded Peter Martin as Secretary/Manager photographed with Mrs. Jenny Pitman. The Moore links with Punchestown go right back to when the late Dan Moore rode there in the Thirties before becoming one of Ireland's most noted National Hunt trainers.

A DREAM REALISED!

Charles Murless, Chief Executive saw a dream realised when the new Punchestown with its £8.7 million complex was officially opened by the Minister of Finance, Charlie McCreevy in April, 1998. (Above) one can see the spaciousness provided for patrons against the background of the new parade ring and imposing stand and (bottom) horses racing for the last time in front of the old stand.

*The Edward O'Grady-trained
Ventana Canyon (Richard Dunwoody) jumping the last
in style on his way to victory in the
Tripleprint Novice Chase at Punchestown '96.*

*The Jim Dreaper-trained Merry Gale (Kevin O'Brien)
taking the last fence on the last circuit on his way
to victory at Punchestown '94.*

*This graphic picture by Caroline Norris captures
the winner Risk of Tunder (Ken Whelan) far side,
and Leagaunel (Jamie Osborne), No 11, sweeping
over the Double Bank at Punchestown '95.*

Limited Edition Print
ARKLE & PAT TAAFFE

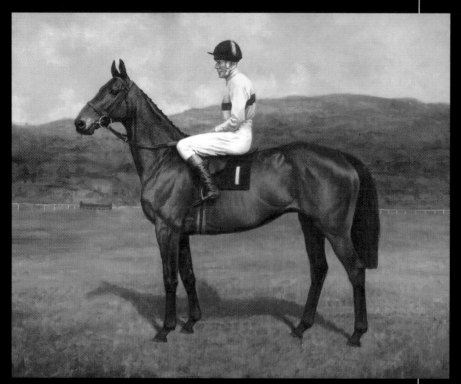

FROM AN OIL PAINTING BY DES SNEE

Thirty six years ago in the closing stages of Arkle's epic battle with Mill House for the 1964 Gold Cup, Sir Peter O'Sullivan comments:

"This is the champion, this is the best we've ever seen."

How prophetic these words were. In the intervening years many horses have been touted as the next Arkle and although we've been lucky enough to see such heroes as Red Rum, Desert Orchid, L'Escargot and Dawn Run, none of them have managed to take the mantle of the greatest. Of course, the name Arkle is synonymous with the legendary Irish trainer Tom Dreaper and the supreme horseman Pat Taaffe, who rode Arkle to all of his great victories.

Des Snee has always been fascinated by Arkle and has portrayed this great chaser many times over the years. It has always been his intention to paint the definitive portrait of this great partnership. Few will argue that he hasn't achieved this. Arkle stands proudly as ever with Pat in the saddle - perhaps at that moment contemplating the fact that he was sitting astride the greatest chaser of them all.

Des Snee has been painting professionally for over twenty years. His work hangs in collections all over the world. In 1993, he was chosen by the owners of Desert Orchid to paint his official portrait; quite an accolade for an Irish artist to paint one of Britain's greatest steeple chasers.

This magnificent print has been produced on 100% cotton paper, using the highest technology available. The edition is limited to only 475 prints worldwide and will in time become a collectors item.

To secure one of these prints, contact

Redmond Fine Art
1, Victoria Terrace
Naas, Co. Kildare

Redmond Fine Art 1 Victoria Terrace Naas Ireland Tel: +353 45 874050

Richard Johnson gave Zafarabad (centre) an inspired ride as he led at the last to hold the challengers of Nomadic (Richard Dunwoody), on Inside and Flagship Uberalles (Tony Mc Coy) right.

Nicky Hederman doesn't seem to mind the drenching downpour after he won the £50,000 B.M.W. Handicap Chase by nine Lengths.

A victory salute from David 'The Duke' Nicholson as he shares with jockey Richard Johnson the joy of victory after Zafarabad had won the I.A.W.S. Championship 4-Year Old Hurdle at Punchestown '98.

*Klarion Davis
(Francis Woods)
jumping the
last in 1996.*

*Francis Woods with the trophy
for the B.M.W. Chase which Klarion
Davis won again in 1997 and
(left) a smiling Tommy Treacy in the
winners enclosure with Native
Upmanship after he had ridden
Arthur Moore's charge to an
impressive victory in the £50,000
Stanley Cooper Champion Novice
Hurdle at Punchestown '98.*

*Tommy Treacy and Native Upmanship
after their win, April '99.*

*ARTHUR MOORE MAINTAINS
FAMILY TRADITION... Arthur has
maintained at Punchestown the
tradition set by his father, the late
Dan Moore as jockey and trainer.
He had two of his finest successes
when Klarion Davis won the B.M.W.
Handicap Chase in successive years
(1996-97). A delighted Moore
gave 'Klarion' the trilby victory
touch after victory in 1996
as had David Thompson shares
the joy of the moment.*

Enda Bolger is carried shoulder-high by fellow jockeys in the winners enclosure. The 36-years-old will now concentrate on his training career. But he will always remember the great moments he enjoyed at Punchestown, especially on Risk of Tunder pictured (above) clearing the Double in 1997.

ENDA BOLGER'S CHAMPAGNE FAREWELL... Enda Bolger with bubbly and the La Touche Cup after his last ride at Punchestown '99 on Risk of Tunder when this amazing 10-year-old in the colours of Sean Connery of James Bond fame won the same for the fifth successive year.

IRELAND'S LEADING SPECIALIST INSURANCE BROKERS

INSURANCES

PERSONAL LINES
- Private Motor Insurance
- Home Insurance
- Personal Effects

LIFE & PENSIONS
- Life Insurance
- Pensions
- Education Fees
- Mortgage Protection
- Permanent Health Insurance

BUS & COACH SPECIALISTS
- Private Hire
- School Transport
- Tour Coaches
- Scheduled Services
- Public / Employer's Liability
- Personal Accident Insurance

CORPORATE
- Business Insurance
- Corporate Risks
- Hotels & Guesthouses

JOHN DUNNE MANAGING DIRECTOR

'Highly - Competitive Quotations on all types of Insurance anywhere in Ireland!'

CAOGA INSURANCES

THE PREMIUM INSURANCE FOR PEOPLE AGED 50 & OVER!

Low cost motor, household and life insurance schemes that make sense if you are aged 50 and over. For information on Caoga Insurance

FREEFONE
1800 730 930

Call us at (045) 876 655 or visit our offices at
J F Dunne Insurances Ltd, 36-37 North Main St., Naas, Co. Kildare.
Tel: (045) 876 655 (30 Lines) Fax: (045) 876 151

Meath trainer Noel Meade, who to the delight of his many admirers had his first-ever winner at Cheltenham 2000 with Sausalito Bay (Paul Carberry) in the Supreme Novices Hurdle recorded a treble at Punchestown '99 with Cardinal Hill, River Pilot and Sydney Twothousand. Meade is pictured (right) in the winners enclosure with Norman Williamson after Sydney Twothousand's win in the Tripleprint Novice Chase.

It was back in 1931 that the late great Tom Dreaper won the Prince of Wales's Plate on Heartbreak Hill and trained Slacker to win the La Touche Cup in 1994. He handed over in 1972 Jim and he quickly maintained the family Punchestown tradition by winning the Champion Novice Hurdle with Good Review and Lough Inagh in successive years and the John Jameson Cup with the latter in '74.

It was back in 1931 that the late great Tom Dreaper won the Prince of Wales's Plate on Heartbreak Hill and trained Slacker to win the La Touche Cup in 1994. He handed over in 1972 Jim and he quickly maintained the family Punchestown tradition by winning the Champion Novice Hurdle with Good Review and Lough Inagh in successive years and the John Jameson Cup with the latter in '74.

Our Promise...

...to provide you with an outstanding professional service thus ensuring your events exceeds your expectations.

MASTERCHEFS

CORPORATE & EVENT CATERERS

We Provide the ultimate in Corporate Catering.

Your Events -

- ***Gala Dinners,***

- ***Company Celebration,***

- ***Corporate Sporting Days,***

- ***Private Marquee Events,***

- ***Corporate Hospitality.***

ASSOCIATION OF
EVENT & CORPORATE
CATERERS

Approved Quality
System

We At Masterchefs realise that no two events are the same and as such our internationally acclaimed chefs strive for culinary excellence at all times. Talk to us today about your occasion, we'll be glad to supply written quotations to the tightest budgets and supply you with our full colour brochure.

Telephone 626 1466 Fax 626 1289 email sales@masterchef.ie

Tony McCoy (left) shows all his power in a finish on His Song (right) as he gets the better of French Ballerina (Graham Bradley) by a head in an epic finish to the Country Pride Champion novice Hurdle at Punchestown '98.

Strong Platinum (Conor O'Dwyre), nearest Camera, on his way to victory over Sound Man (Charlie Swan) in the Bank of Ireland Novice Chase at Punchestown '95.

Mouse Morris, the successful trainer

Meath trainer Michael Cunningham, and his great patron and sporting owner Herb Strong, have enjoyed some great moments at Punchestown with Derrymoyle, pictured nearest camera, in the hands of Tony McCoy winning the Champion Stayers Hurdle in 1999 from Paddy's Return (Norman Williamson) which was third. Derrymoyle also triumphed in the same race '98, and in '96 took the Davenport Hotel Tipperkevin Hurdle.

Istabraq and Charlie Swan take the last in champion style and go on for a clear-cut three-and-a-half lengths win from English Challenger Decoupage, (not in picture) and Limestone Lad (Tony McCoy). The Shell Champion Hurdle had a prize-fund of £100,000.

THOSE ISTABRAQ DAYS OF GLORY... J.P. McManus acknowledges the cheers of the crowd at Punchestown '99 as he receives the the trophy from the Shell Chairman and managing director of Shell Ireland after Istabraq had won the managerial running of the race on the last day of the first four-day festival meeting.

J.P.M. McManus and Charlie Swan recieve their trophies from John O'Brien, Marketing and Sales Director, after Cardinal Hill had won the opening day of Punchestown '99.

*CHARLIE SWAN, JP McMANUS
and AIDAN O'BRIEN...
The genius of Aidan O'Brien
has made possible Istabraq's
three successive victories in the
Smurfit Champion Hurdle
and the scintillating successes
also at Punchestown and
other venues.*

*J.P. McManus and his wife, Noreen with the
trophy they received after Istabraq had won
the Stanley Cook Champion Novice Hurdle
at Punchestown '97 by nine lengths.*

*(Above) The Chris Rourke trained Grimes,
named after J.P's good friend Eamon Grimes,
who led Limerick to victory in the 1973
All-Ireland Senior Hurling final, triumphed
at Punchestown '97 in the Murphys Irish
Stout Champion Four-Year-Old Hurdle.
J.P. has reason to smile as he is presented
with the imposing rtophy.*

Estate Agents & Valuers
to the Thoroughbred County

Over the years Jordan Town and Country Estate Agents
have built up a reputation for selling some of Kildare's most
famous country property, sporting estates and stud farms.

With the increasing globalisation of the property market
we are superbly positioned to source exceptional
investment opportunities for our increasing clients
both nationally and internationally.

TOWN AND COUNTRY ESTATE AGENTS

Jordan

**JORDAN
TOWN & COUNTRY
ESTATE AGENTS,**
FIAVI, MIREF,
Edward Street, Newbridge,
Co. Kildare
Tel: 00+353 45 433550
Fax: 00+353 45 434122
email: jordanau@indigo.ie
www.jordan-auctioneers.ie

*J.P. McManus has also named horses
after other very good friends of his from
the 1973 Limerick Champion team, namely
Pat Hartigan is pictured (left) chatting
with the Minister of finance Charlie McCreevy
at Punchestown '98.*

*THREE ALL-TIME GREATS...
Tommy Carberry, Frank Berry
and Jonjo O'Neill before
they rode in a Charity Race
at Punchestown '91.*

one racecourse

one printer

Anglo
Printers

Mell Industrial Estate, Drogheda, Co. Louth.
Telephone 041 9835000   *Fax* 041 9835541   *ISDN* 041 9870206
email anglo@indigo.ie   *web* http://kol.ie/ANGLO

You've Arrived. Your journey made comfortable by a driving position forever sealed in the memory of the luxury, leathered seats. Eased by the finger-tip control of the air conditioning, electric sliding sun-roof and integrated phone on the multi-function steering wheel, and enjoyed through the quality of the multi-play CD sounds and an on board computerised information display. A journey made safe by the responsive feel of the five speed 'Steptronic' Automatic Adaptive Transmission System, the secure handling of the Automatic Traction Control, ABS, and the silent assurance of the driver, passenger and side impact airbags. A journey of effortless, driving pleasure embodied in the thirty-two-valved, vee-eight-engined, two hundred and eighty six brake-horse-powered, seventy-odd-thousand-quids-worth of beautiful, understated class. Today's motoring technology ensuring tomorrow's great residual value.

Arrange a journey in **the new 7 Series BMW.**

THE ULTIMATE DRIVING MACHINE

Motor Import Limited, BMW House, J.F.K. Drive, Naas Road, Dublin 12.
Telephone: 01 240 5666. Fax: 01 450 8509. email: info@bmw.ie Internet : http://www.bmw.ie

The Charly Mann - trained 'Celibate' (Richard Dunwoody) jumping last from Direct Rule (Norman Williamson), who made a mistake and Celebrate went on to take the B.M.W. Chase.

12

EIGHT ENGLISH-TRAINED WINNERS AT PUNCHESTOWN '99 TOM JONES BLAZED A TRAIL FOR A DECADE

The 20th century closed with English-trained horses landing eight races at Punchestown '99 - the clearest indication of how the appeal of the meeting has been cemented for British trainers and that they are willing to send over contenders who have the credentials to enter the winner's enclosure and win spontaneous and generous applause in the process.

It's amazing how matters have changed in the course of close on 40 years.

Honour Bound, winner earlier of Division 1 of Cheltenham's Gloucestershire Hurdle, gave English stables their first post-War victory at Punchestown in the third running of the Martin Mahony Champion Novice Hurdle, in 1963. Trained by Fred Rimell and ridden by Terry Biddlecombe, the five-year-old had no difficulty in winning at 7/4, generous odds considering that the Irish challengers had been defeated in all three Divisions of the Gloucestershire Hurdle.

Tom MacGinty, who was for close on 30 years Racing Correspondent of the *Irish Independent*, and was present to report on Honour Bound's triumph made the point that the expected deluge of English challengers did not materialise at subsequent Kildare Festivals. The only British trainer to travel in any strength and meet with success was H. Thompson Jones, the popular Newmarket handler known to all and sundry as Tom Jones.

The Nickey Henderson - trained Katarino (Mick Fitzgerald) jumping last as he went on for victory over Golden Rule (Richard Dunwoody) in the I.A.W.S. champion four year old Hurdle at Punchestown '99.

He and his stable jockey Stan Mellor, a frequent visitor to this country, won the 1966 Downshire Handicap Hurdle with Red Tears; the following year's Martin Mahony Champion Novice Hurdle with Chorus and in 1970 brought off a double with Marcia's Mark and Frozen Alive.

Tingle Creek

The latter won the Champion Novice Hurdle and the following year the combination gained their third success in that event with Ouzo, but Tom Jones' most spectacular Punchestown winner was surely the American-bred speed horse Tingle Creek, who in 1974 with David Mould in the saddle and revelling on the fast ground, gave an exhilarating front-running display in the Drogheda Handicap Chase. Despite a mistake two out, he beat Skymas, a local hero, by six lengths. Tingle Creek was giving the runner-up 16lbs. - some performance considering that Skymas went on to win the N.H. Two Miles Champion Chase (now the Queen Mother Champion Chase) in 1976 and '77.

Nicholson Equals Score

That was Tom Jones' sixth and final Punchestown winner, and it was only in 1997 that compatriot David Nicholson equalled his score (and subsequently went on to beat it). The late date of the fixture and the consequent risk of fast going, did not encourage travellers from overseas, but a more important contributary factor was prize money. The stakes had been raised over the years, but not enough to encourage British owners and trainers to extend their best horses' seasons to take on the Irish on their own ground.

Then with the spectacular increase in prize-money, due to generous sponsorship from leading concerns, there was a dramatic change and trainers saw Punchestown as the ideal venue to bid for rich prizes with good ground specialists.

David 'The Duke' Nicholson spotted an opportunity in 1987 for High Plains in the BMW Champion Novice Hurdle. Richard Dunwoody rode and High Plains, improving from a promising fourth at Cheltenham, won well. Neville Callaghan took up the running in 1989 and 1990 winning the Guinness Trophy 4-y-o Hurdle and Waterford Crystal Hotel Handicap with Royal Derbi; and Oliver Sherwood, no stranger to Punchestown, having spent some of his formative years with Arthur Moore, put his spoke in to lift the 1991 Champion Novice Hurdle with Young Pokie ridden by Jamie Osborne.

The Richard Foley-trained Noyan (Norman Williamson) runs away from the last fence to win the 1997 Heineken Gold Cup as Corvet (Trevor Hogan) falls.

Backed from 10/1 in the morning to 2/1 favourite, Postage Stamp (Mark Dwyer) in the colours of Paddy O'Donnell brought off a 'marvelous touch' according to trainer Ferdy Murphy at Punchestown '95

Staunch Supporter

Since then - and right up to 1999 - David Nicholson, now retired, became a staunch supporter of the Festival meeting. "Much has changed" he said in the course of an interview with Graham Dench of the "Racing Post", "since my first visit back in 1987, and I think I can honestly say that in just about every respect it has changed for the better".

"Not that there was a problem the first time I came - far from it. I thoroughly enjoyed myself then, and I've had a marvellous time every time I've been back".

"Every one of Ireland's Festivals no doubt has its attractions, but the atmosphere is as good at Punchestown as at any I've been to, and the racing is different class. What's more, the prize-money leaves nothing to be desired".

"Then, of course, there is the legendary Irish hospitality, provided not only for owners and trainers, but also for horses and lads. The new facilities on offer now are unbelievable. I take my hat off to Charlie Murless and his team for the marvellous job they've done".

"As you can see, Punchestown holds any number of attractions, but I suppose what distinguished it for me always from Cheltenham and Aintree was the lack of pressure. Cheltenham was all pressure for me and to a lesser extent so was Aintree".

"At Punchestown the pressure was off and I could unwind, because almost everything was done for me and the season was drawing to a close".

"After that initial success in 1987 I saw the time arrive when the competition got hotter and hotter. It was always hard enough beating the Irish on their own soil without having rivals from a dozen or more top British stables to contend with.

"The first time I sent horses over in numbers was back in 1993 (I had moved then into Jackdaw's Castle in 1992 and stepped up the whole operation a couple of gears), and I'll never forget the time we had. Viking Flagship was our main hope, and he won not just once, but twice.

"I've very seldom run a horse twice in 48 hours, as I did then, but Viking Flagship had missed both Cheltenham and Aintree on account of the ground.

The Flagships Double

"On the first day of the meeting 'The Flagship' was a warm favourite for the BMW Drogheda Handicap Chase with only 10st 7lb, and he won well enough, without being over-impressive. Two days later I pulled him out again for the Bank of Ireland Novices Chase and he won again, and this time in style, beating Antonin at 4/1, (Richard Dunwoody was the successful rider on both occasions).

Celebrations

"He was definitely better on the Thursday than he had been on the Tuesday, but I'm not sure I can say the same for myself. As you can imagine, we'd celebrated long and hard with owner Graham Roach and his party after 'The Flagship's' win on Tuesday, and we hadn't exactly been abstinent on the Wednesday.

"The scenes when 'The Flagship' went in for the second time were just unbelievable. And we were due in Newmarket that night for the Guineas meeting! How we made it I'll never know.

"Since then I have been lucky enough to enjoy further success with Billygoat Gruff in the Heineken Gold Cup in 1996 and then with both Midnight Legend in the Country Pride Champion Novices' Hurdle and Arctic Camper in the Doncaster Bloodstock Sales Champion Bumper in 1997, when we also had three seconds and a third".

In 1998 Nicholson won the I.A.W.S. Champion 4-y-o Hurdle with Zafarabad (R. Johnson) in a blanket finish by a neck and a neck from Nomadic and Flagship Uberalles.

How fitting that his last hurrah as a trainer to Punchestown in 1999 should see him take the Stayers Hurdle with Anzum who had earlier won at Cheltenham.

Truly International

By now Punchestown had become a truly International Festival. The immense effort made by the Executive and the Racing Authorities in 1992 had certainly paid off handsomely. Apart from the dramatic increase in prize-money, an all-out effort was made to attract overseas runners and it met with almost instant success. Close on 20 horses arrived from Britain. Martin Pipe and Peter Scudamore lifted two races with Milford Quay and Aquilifier and Mark Tompkins won the Guinness Trophy with the 4-y-o Staunch Friend ridden by Steve Smith-Eccles.

Nicky Henderson has been another staunch supporter of Punchestown down the years and in 1993 he won the Berkeley Court Handicap Hurdle on Thinking Twice with Richard Dunwoody in the saddle.

The Lambourn trainer, whose name will always be linked with See You Then, Remittance Man and Tsarevich and who enjoyed a smashing Cheltenham '99 with four winners, Tiutchev (Arkle Chase), Marlborough (National Hunt Chase), Bacchanell (Stayers Hurdle), and Stormyfairweather (Cathcart Cup), admits that Punchestown is one meeting that he looks forward to with great eagerness each year.

Not Good For The Liver

"We have been coming to Punchestown for many years now and its appeal never lessens for us", he told me. "We have great times with Johnny and Jessica Harrington and their friends. There's the golf and the racing and what the Irish describe so aptly as 'the craic' and all told it's a week that invariably leaves us with a lot of happy memories".

"But the better the memories, the harder it is on the system. Yes, Punchestown is not good for the liver!", he added with a smile.

Henderson said that sponsorship had greatly increased the prize-money on offer at Punchestown. There are prizes now well worth challenging for, especially if you have the type of contender fit to take its place in the field.

He added that Punchestown also offered excellent opportunities to trainers who might have a horse that produced its best in the Spring. "It comes at the ideal time in the racing calendar after Cheltenham and Aintree."

Nicky Henderson recorded a double at Punchestown '99 with Cheltenham winner, Katarino in the I.A.W.S. Champion 4-y-o Hurdle and Blue Royal in the Ellier Developments Ltd. 4-y-o Hurdle, both ridden to victory by Mick Fitzgerald.

Connot Stay Away

North Yorkshire-based Ferdy Murphy who was assistant to Bill Durkan in the glory days of Anaglog's Daughter, admits that there is no way he can stay away from the Punchestown Festival.

"The three days sort out the men from the boys and it is an ideal end-of-season Festival for everybody", was how he put it in an interview with English racing correspondent and writer, Claude Duval. "The meeting caters for English trainers in so many ways. First, you can almost be certain of top-of-the-ground going. That's very important if you have a horse who has been crying out for fast ground but has been sidelined by a wet Spring. Secondly, the prize-money is unbelievable. At Punchestown the cash rewards are terrific and stand up well to the rewards available at Cheltenham and Aintree.

"I Love It"

"Thirdly, there is the craic. If you go racing and you don't enjoy yourself at Punchestown, then you don't deserve to keep breathing. I love it. People ask me where the action is after racing and I tell them: 'Just follow the crowd'".

And in Ferdy Murphy's case, that means heading with his friends for his favourite racing pub - and the hours will pass quickly in the sheer enjoyment of it all.

"Lucky Track For Me"

"I rode at Punchestown and it was always a lucky track for me. Since I've been back as a trainer it has also been very fortunate for me. When Mark Dwyer won on Paddy O'Donnell's Postage Stamp a few years back it was a marvellous touch. We backed him from 10-1 in the morning down to 2/1 favourite".

In 1997, Paddy's Return (Norman Williamson) won the I.A.W.S. Centenary Year Champion Hurdle for Murphy.

"Punchestown has really taken off in recent years and with the new complex it is even better. As a boy I can remember that it was always the highlight of the farmers' racing year. They had all the

"I saw the time arrive when the competition got hotter and hotter"-David Nicholson. Midnight Legend (Richard Johnson) at left winning the Country Pride Champion Novices Hurdle for the Nicholson stable in 1997 and (below) Big Matt (Mick Fitzgerald) winning the B.M.W. Chase in 1998 for Nicky Henderson.

The Nigel Triston-Davies-trained Mahler (Carl Llewellyn) (at left) at an early stage of the 1998 Heineken Gold Cup which he went on to win by five lenghts.

ploughing done and the corn was in. They could afford to unwind and Punchestown was the place to do it," added Murphy.

Rough Quest Wins

In 1995, the Castlemartin Stud Pat Taaffe Handicap Chase saw victory going to Rough Quest trained by English-based Donegal born, Terry Casey and ridden by Mick Fitzgerald. The nine-year-old had come a second time, having been almost put out of the race at the penultimate fence, Casey was enthusiastic about the 1996 Aintree Grand National. Rough Quest did

not let him down, horse and rider going on to give an immaculate exhibition, bar a mild deviation in the closing stages.

Apart from the successes recorded by regulars David 'The Duke' Nicholson (Anzum) and Nicky Henderson (Katarino and Blue Royal), Punchestown '99 showed in the other British-trained winners how more trainers from across-Channel were being attracted to challenge for its prizes including some who were completely new to the scene.

Celibate (Charlie Mann), Bouchasson (P.J. Hobbs), Castle Mane (Mrs C. Bailey), Jocks Cross (Miss Venetia Williams), all entered the winner's enclosure with their charges.

The Anglo-Irish rivalry at Punchestown is now comparable with that at the Cheltenham Festival meeting and it's what adds that extra spice and bite to the showpiece races in particular. Long may it continue thus.

*Willie Mullins and his father pictured in 1988 when Willie was
champion amateur rider and Paddy champion National Hunt trainer.*

13

THE MULLINS DYNASTY PLAY DOMINANT ROLE IN EIGHTIES AND NINETIES

P addy Mullins, who might well be described as the grand old man of the Irish training profession, celebrated his 80th birthday early in 2000.

He was still turning out the winners from his Goresbridge, Co. Kilkenny establishment and at the time of writing in late February '99, he had produced seventeen winners from ten horses.

It was back in 1953 that Paddy Mullins had his first winner at Punchestown - a horse called Flash Parade 11, which he rode himself to victory in the La Touche Cup.

Forty-five years on at Punchestown in the last year of the 20th century, he turned out Hurry Bob to win the bumper on the first day and then on the third day hen he also took the bumper with Better Think Again and on the final day he was victorious with Clifdon Fog in the Lawlors of Naas Poitin Still Handicap Chase.

A treble at such a highly-competitive meeting and with such powerful opposition from across-Channel proved that the Master of Goresbridge had not lost his touch for turning out the winners.

One Generation To The Next

We have already seen how the Beasleys, the Osbornes and the Floods have at different peiods dominated the Great Festival. The late Tom Dreaper, who won the Prince of Wales plate on Hearbreak Hill in 1931, and trained Slacker to win the La Touche in 1942, handed over to his son Jim in 1972 and he promptly won the Champion Novice Hurdle with Good Review and Lough Inagh in successive years, and the John Jameson Cup with the latter in '74.

Three generations of Hydes and Taaffes have been associated with winners at Punchestown's Festival; the O'Grady's, the Moores and the Walshs have figured as owners, trainers and riders, immersed in the National Hunt sport. P.J. Prendergast Jnr and his brother Kevin, whose father won the Drogheda Plate with Melman, ridden by Connie Eddery, in 1950, before becoming completely absorbed in Flat racing, have visited the winner's enclosure. So too Dermot Weld and one cannot leave out the Hartys, Capt. Cyril and his sons Eddie and the late John. Cyril, an officer in the National Army won the last running of the Military Cup on Santos in 1922.

During the latter days of the 20th century we have witnessed the emergence of a new dynamic force in the shape of Aidan O'Brien, who in '95, '96 and '97 picked off the Murphy's Irish Stout Champion 4-y-o Hurdle and the Stanley Cooker Champion Novice Hurdle twice, the latter in '97 with the brilliant new Champion Hurdler of 1998, Istabraq, who the following year won the inaugural running of the Shell Champion Hurdle.

The Mullins Family

Few, however, would dispute the contention that the Mullins family has been the reigning dynasty at Punchestown during the Eighties and Nineties.

By the Sixties, the Doninga, Co. Kilkenny stable had developed into a serious contender at the highest level. Vulpine and Paddy Mullins' first

Cheltenham winner Herring Gull, won the Irish Nationals of 1967 and '68. Dim Wit, winner of Punchestown's John Jameson Chase in 1971, won the Irish National in the following season.

With four sons, George, Willie, Tony and Tom and one daughter, Sandra, all slipping into the Doninga team, things began to hum, and nowhere more constantly than at Punchestown.

Willie, Tony and Tom have all ridden winners over the course, and the first two named, already well established as trainers, have also saddled winners at the festival.

Judging by how quickly Willie Mullins has made the headlines as a trainer at Cheltenham's Festival, where he rode three winners (in five seasons he was either outright or joint champion amateur rider in Ireland) it was obvious that he was going to be a force at Punchestown considering the fire power at his disposal.

FROM A FIRST WINNER IN '53 TO A TREBLE 46 YEARS LATER AT PUNCHESTOWN '99... Paddy Mullins, at right, who celebrated his 80th birthday early in 2000, in the winners enclosure at Punchestown '99 with the Hill family, his wife Maureen and jockey, Tommy Treacy after Clifdon Fog had provided one leg of a fabulous treble.

*One of three races which the front running mare Grable
won for Paddy Mullins at Punchestown in sucessive years.
Here Tony Mullins triumphs in style in 1988.*

With a more amenable build and weight, Tony became a professional jockey, was joint champion in Ireland in 1984 and rode some of his most memorable races for his father at this famous Kildare meet.

In 1983 he won the BMW Champion Novice Hurdle on Dawn Run and the Guinness Handicap Chase on Pearlstone, who had provided him with his first winner, as an amateur rider, in a 14 furlong maiden at Tramore in 1979, and who won the Cri Help Champion 4-y-o Hurdle ridden by Sean Tracy. Pearlstone was Paddy Mullins' third winner of the Guinness Hnadicap Chase, following Kilbracken Money and Irish Grand National winner Luska, mount of Tommy Finn. Twelve months later, Lantern Lodge and Tony provided the trainer with his fourth Guinness Handicap in five years.

Paddy and Tony, who over the next three seasons completed a hat-trick with the front funning mare, Grabel, winner initially of the Champion 4-y-o Hurdle and in 1988 and '89 of the Bookmakers Handicap Hurdle. Tony Mullins subsequently took out a trainer's licence and reduced his number of rides, but he trained and rode Doran's Town Lad to win the Mont Clare Hotel Hurdle in 1992.

Pearlstone (Tony Mullins) winning at Punchestown '83 after surviving this mistake at the last.

Mr. Tom Mullins made his Punchestown mark in the Doncaster Champion Bumper on Noble Thyne in 1996.

14

THE NEW PUNCHESTOWN

Charles Murless is the man at the helm as Chief Executive who shouldered with commendable coolness and strength of character the immense responsibilities of seeing the creation of the 'new Punchestown' with its magnificent £8.75 million complex, formally opened by the Minister for Finance, Charles McCreevy in April, 1998.

No one could envy him, as he realised from the moment the contractors moved into Punchestown in August '97 that it was a race against the clock. But when you take into account the fact that 87,000 racegoers attended the Festival meeting over the four days in 1999, you quickly come to realise how necessary it was that action was taken by the Punchestown Committee at that particular time.

He was well groomed for the task, succeeding Mrs. Joan Moore who was an outstanding achiever in her seven years (1987-'94) as Secretary-Manager and who played a key role with Bord Failte personnel in Britain, like Margaret Cahill and Mark Rowlette, in encouraging British trainers to support the meeting as it graduated into a true international Festival.

Charles Murless had been Marketing Director at Doncaster during the tenure of John Sanderson as Chief Executive. Together they saw through the transformation of the track into the model racecourse it is today and they also saw the staging of the first-ever Sunday race meeting in Britain. Prior to his period at Doncaster, he had been attached to Goffs.

The sunken parade ring, an integral part of the 'new Punchestown' showing Istabraq parading before he won at the 1998 meeting. Looking on are John Magnier, with Aidan and Anne-Marie O'Brien.

He arrived at Punchestown as Manager but when it became obvious the 'new' Punchestown would have to be created almost from scratch, his title changed to Chief Executive as the tasks facing him extended far, far more than simply supervising normal race days and included the ongoing development of Punchestown as the National Equestrian and Field Sports Centre.

Son of Stuart Murless

He is son of the late Stuart Murless, who was an outstanding trainer and is best remembered for the Classic winners he put through his hands, Nocturnal Spree, winner of the English 1,000 Guineas in 1975 and Pampapaul, winner of the Irish 2,000 Guineas in 1977 and French and Irish St. Leger winners, Sicilian Prince and Royal Highway. He was, of course, brother of master trainer, Sir Noel Murless, who had a succession of Classic winners to his name and whose daughter, Julie Cecil, formerly married to Henry Cecil, carries on a proud tradition at Newmarket.

He is married to the very personable Rhona Blake, a Director with Fleishman-Hillard Saunders, the Dublin-based Public Relations Consultants. Their first child was appropriately named Stu, after his grandfather.

A view of the enclosure area as seen at Punchestown '99.

From his days attached to a pony club, when he was first brought by his parents to the Spring meeting, Punchestown has retained a deep significance for Charles Murless and he does not hide his affection for everything associated with it. "Punchestown has stood as a very special place and from my youthful days I have nothing but the happiest memories of going racing here", he told me.

Now, as we advance into the new Millennium he knows that new generations will derive the same enjoyment, and he likes to think that he will have contributed to giving them the kind of amenities that earlier generations could never have envisaged.

The main Grand Stand as a viewing area for the races was already there - and on the back of it was erected a three-storey building incorporating on the ground floor a spacious betting hall, bars and Tote outlets; on the second floor the Hunt Bar and on the third the private suites. Eleven of these were easily disposed of on a twenty-year basis. The same has been the case with a further 10 private suites in the newly completed Panoramic Stand, situated on the left of the main stand, with additional covered viewing for many thousands of racegoers. This three-storey structure is the principal element of Phase 2 and also accommodates the "Panoramic Restaurant", which will provide state of the art comfort with table top viewing and betting outlets as well as an unparrelled view of the racecourse.

Sunken Parade Ring

A centre-piece of the complex is the sunken parade ring which is overlooked from the back of the main Grandstand.

And going hand-in-hand with this is the saddling-up area with weigh room, offering racegoers a perfect view of the horses being saddled before they enter the parade ring and a new restaurant-bar building. Beside the entrance building are sited the entrance marquees and trade stands.

Completion of Phase One

1998 saw the completion of just one phase of a very ambitious Development Plan. Initially, the emphasis was to ensure that patrons would no long be at the mercy of the weather.

In the reserved enclosure is to be found the Marquee area answering all the requirements of hospitality for companies entertaining guests over racing days.

The red-brick facade gives just the right touch to the new Grand Stand building.

Whereas in the past, Punchestown could be bleak and a test for even the hardiest of souls in winter when there was rain on the wind, one no longer has to brave the elements while viewing the racing in comfort from 'inside' the new Grand Stands - and you can have a bet or a drink all under cover. The days of standing under a gable end while sheltering from the elements are gone.

After the huge success of Punchestown '99 - extended to four days for the first time - the management could easily have rested on their laurels. Not so. Work has ploughed ahead with further work on the car parks to ensure that there would be no repetition of the nightmare problems that arose during the deluge of rain that hit the track in 1998 and a further Phase 3 development is at the final planning stage involving the construction and development of an agricultural exhibition and event centre at Punchestown.

New Chasing and Hurdle Tracks

Charles Murless, however, is equally conscious that to provide a four day Festival on acceptable going, whatever the weather, means additional racing ground. As he has said so often in the past "no track, no racing", and with that in mind new 'chasing and hurdle tracks have been provided, and an extensive drainage system put in place.

Moveable fences will be utilised on the new chasing course - they will also provide the last four fences on the existing track - further extending the management's options.

No other course in the country is geared to provide such a variety of equine entertainment. Under National Hunt Rules alone apart from the accepted norm of present day steeplechasing and hurdling, the Festival offers the last opportunities, apart from some point-to-points, for hunters to compete over banks, and then of course there is the extremely popular cross-country chase over a mix of fences on a criss-cross track.

Outside of the big three-day Spring Festival meeting and the other important fixtures during the National Hunt season, Punchestown now stages racing as well during the Flat season. This is an area which it can, in the future expand further as it now has a track that meets all the necessary requirements.

Florida Pearl (Richard Dunwoody) graced the 1999 meeting in the Heineken Gold Cup but had to give best to Imperial Call (Ruby Walsh), the 1996 Cheltenham Gold Cup winner

National Equestrian Centre

It was decided from an early stage that Punchestown should not, as far as possible, be merely a state-of-the-art course used exclusively for racing. The equestrian tradition has always been strong, going right back over half-a-century.

When one thinks of those who had the vision to fully support the creation of the 'new Punchestown', one must not overlook that role of Dermot Cox, a true Punchestown stalwart who was deeply committed to its future and well-being.

And, of course, James Osborne, the Chairman has been a dynamic force from the outset in his determination that no stone would be left unturned to make Punchestown a model for other tracks to follow.

Jessica Harrington, one of Ireland's leading lady trainers to-day, who trained Ferbert Junior to win the Bradstock Insurance Novice Chase at Punchestown '99, was the top eventer in the country for a period of almost 20 years. She was a member of the Irish team that competed at the Los Angeles Olympics in 1984. She was the best Irish competitor at Badminton, she admits that it was, perhaps, the high point of her three-day eventing career. Her father Brigadier B. J. Fowler was an outstanding international polo player.

Punchestown has been declared the National Equestrian Centre.

Punchestown was declared the National Centre for Equestrian and Field Sports of Ireland

A sum of £1.5 million was received from the European Regional Development Fund through Bord Failte and this has been utilised to build an all-weather show-jumping area of the highest international standard. German born Herman Deckek, recognised as the world authority on all weather surfaces, was engaged with the brief to ensure that the surface of the arena would pass the sternest test.

There is an ever-growing interest in cross-country riding which leads on in turn to an interest in following the hunt. Some people may not have sufficient proficiency in riding to go hunting but it is possible to graduate from cross-country riding, firstly acquiring the basic skills and then progressing to the obstacles in natural hunting country.

Hunting is very much part of the tourist industry in this country. It appeals particularly to foreign visitors, especially from Continental countries and the United States, who love to be able to say that they hunted with the renowned Irish Hunts, which have a wealth of tradition behind them. None having a longer or greater tradition than the Kildare Hunt itself.

In a word then, the ambitious development that saw the opening of the £8.75 million complex in 1988 has given a dual benefit both in the field of racing and in the arena of international eventing. Punchestown, with its 500 acres and sited so conveniently near Dublin, has entered the era when, more and more, it will play a crucial role in advancing the aims of the Irish tourist industry - and in a very important field at that.

INFLUX OF BRITISH RACING ENTHUSIASTS

Over 5,000 racing enthusiasts from Britain now attend the Punchestown Festival meeting each Spring and the figure is on the increase all the time.

It is now, according to Betty O'Connell, promotions and Tourism Manager of the Irish Horseracing Authority, become one of the most popular meetings of all with the racing fraternity in Britain. "It has reached the point that when people are pulling out of their hotels and guesthouses at the end of one Festival meeting, they automatically book for the following year", she said. "It has been a boon to Naas and other centres in Co. Kildare, and the business people will tell you that you cannot but be impressed by the amount of sterling in circulation".

Punchestown is a 'must' now in the racing packages of Ireland devised by tour operators in Britain - without question the National Hunt meeting with the greatest appeal.

Betty O'Connell recalls that back in 1990-91 Bord Failte in the UK, in conjunction with the racing interest in Ireland, looked at how racing could be developed as an integral part of the tourism industry. Punchestown was chosen as the ideal fixture to be promoted as a major Spring Festival, following on Cheltenham and Aintree, and yet outside the peak travel time of Easter.

Bord Failte in Ireland has worked hand-in-hand with the Racing Authorities here and have engaged in many joint overseas promotions. During the last few years the "Horseracing in Ireland" stand at both the November and March festivals in Cheltenham and also at other venues in the UK has gone from strength to strength. General information on racing in Ireland and brochures highlighting Punchestown, and indeed all the other Festival meetings, are available to British visitors to Ireland. The majority of racegoers now have their individual brochures ideal for these promotions. "There is an ever increasing demand for such information from the British racing enthusiasts, who simply love the special friendly atmosphere of the Irish race-meetings and the mingling in the bars and enclosures", said Betty O'Connell, they want to come back time and time again".

Betty O'Connell's own contribution to promoting the influx of racing enthusiasts from Britain to Punchestown cannot be too highly praised.

CONTRIBUTORS

Raynond Smith

Well-known racing writer, Raymond Smith was author of a number of highly-acclaimed best-selling books, including *Vincent O'Brien: The Master of Ballydoyle* (1991) and a revised and updated edition *Vincent O'Brien: The Man and The Legend* in 1997 to coincide with Vincent's 80th birthday; also *Tigers of Turf 1994*, *Better One Day as a Lion 1996* and *The High Rollers of The Turf* (1992) and a new edition in 1999 to coincide with the launch of the video of the prize- winning film, *Murphy's Stroke*, starring Niall Toibin and Pierse Brosnan of James Bond fame.

Raymond Smith was editor of the *Irish Racing Annual* which celebrates its 25th birthday in the year 2000. Raymond Smith died on 2nd April 2000.

Ashley McDermott

A senior-staff member at Punchestown Racecourse, Ashley acted as research assistant and project co-ordinator with specialist responsibilities for advertising and promotion.

Con Costello

Dr Con Costello has published extensively on the history of County Kildare. For thirty years he edited the *Journal of County Kildare Archaeological Society*, and he has contributed a series on local history to the *Leinster Leader* for almost twenty years. His books include *Kildare: Saints Soldiers & Horsemen* and *A Most Delightful Station: The British Army on the Curragh of Kildare, 1855-1922*, as well as *Botany Bay*, a study of the transportation of convicts to Australia, and *Ireland and the Holy Land*, an account of the involvement of Irish people in the Levant.

Caroline Norris

Caroline Norris specialises in racing and bloodstock photography. Well known in the equestrian world, she is retained by many publications including *The Racing Post*, *The Irish Field* and the *Irish Racing Annual*. Caroline is based in Kildare and works with many leading breeders and trainers as well as covering Irish and international racing events.

Ivy Green Pat Taffe afte winning Galway Hurdle 19

INDEX